FAITH FOR FIERY TRIALS

Testimonies That Will Ignite the Fire in Your Soul and Increase Your Faith in God

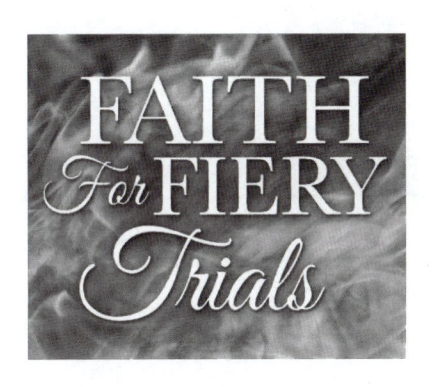

Nicole S. Mason

FAITH FOR FIERY TRIALS

Testimonies That Will Ignite the Fire in Your Soul and Increase Your Faith in God

All Rights Reserved.
Copyright © 2018 by Nicole S. Mason, Esq.
Published by J. Mosley Publishing Company
Co-Author Photos by Jackie Hicks
Book Cover Design by Sherilyn Bennett
Editors: Minister Beverly Lucas and Elder Angela Thornton
Book Layout by Dr. Angela D. Massey

All rights reserved. No part of this publication may be reproduced, distributed or transmitted in any form or by any means, including photocopying, recording, or other electronic or mechanical methods, without the prior written permission of the publisher, except in the case of brief quotations embodied in critical reviews and certain other noncommercial uses permitted by copyright law. For permission requests, write to the publisher, addressed "Attention: Permissions Coordinator," at the address below.

Strategies For Success, LLC
P.O. Box 29427
Washington, DC 20017
www.nicolesmason.com
(240) 343-4742

The following translations have been used:
Scripture quotations marked NKJV are from the New King James Version of the Bible. Copyright © 1979, 1980, 1982 by Thomas Nelson, Inc., publishers. Used by permission.

Scripture quotations marked NIV are from the Holy Bible, New International Version® NIV®. Copyright © 1973, 1978, 1984 by International Bible Society. Used by permission of Zondervan Publishing House. All rights reserved.

Scripture quotations marked The Message are from The Message: The Bible in Contemporary English. Copyright © 1993, 1994, 1995, 1996, 2000, 2001, 2002. Used by permission of NavPress Publishing Group.

Scripture quotations marked NLT are from The New Living Translation. Copyright © 1996, 2004. Used by permission of Tyndale House Publishers, Inc., Wheaton, IL 60189. All rights reserved.

Ordering Information
Quantity sales and special discounts are available on quantity purchases by corporations, associations, and others. For details, contact the "Special Sales Department" at the address above.
Printed in USA

Faith For Fiery Trials: Testimonies That Will Ignite The Fire In Your Soul And Increase Your Faith In God/Nicole S. Mason, Esquire

ISBN 10: 1720694141
ISBN 13: 978-1720694144

Dedication

This book is dedicated in loving memory to:

Andrew David Dantzler
May 5, 1998 – July 8, 2016

Erin Ashleigh Mercer
February 1, 1988 – June 15, 2004

Elijah Muhammad Turner, Jr.
January 23, 1990 – August 8, 2011

Foreword

The Word of God compassionately assures us that, "We are pressed on every side, but not crushed; perplexed, but not in despair; persecuted, but not abandoned; struck down, but not destroyed" (2 Corinthians 4:8-9 NIV). Indeed, all of us experience times of adversity, trials and tribulation in our lives but those trials often lead to our greatest testimonies. As demonstrated in *Faith for Fiery Trials*, our individual trials position us to exercise the utmost, deep-rooted faith, belief, and reliance on the Creator even through the most unexpected, challenging circumstances and life events that our human spirit can't begin to comprehend. *Faith for Fiery Trials* is a soul-stirring compilation of real life stories that highlight the urgency of turning to God and His Word for strength, comfort, and peace during such trials.

The visionary of this potent book compilation, Elder Nicole S. Mason, is a God-fearing woman and leader who is intentional about transparently sharing the trials she has personally faced in her life journey as a testimony for others of what God can and will usher you through. She continues to blaze the trail and set the example for other women to courageously share their testimony as she has done in this brilliant written work.

As demonstrated in the compelling stories of each co-author of *Faith for Fiery Trials*, when we are faced with trials the enemy will attempt to insert doubt and questions into our minds about God's love and His goodness. We can choose to allow that doubt to settle into our spirit and ask, "Why me?" or we can grow from our trials, increase our faith in God, and ask, "How can I be faithful in the midst of this trial?" We can allow adversity to break us down and make us bitter, or we can let it refine us and make us spiritually stronger. The reality is that spiritual growth can often be achieved more readily though trials and adversity than it can through comfort and tranquility.

In each of the stories that you read in this compilation—including stories of grief due to the loss of a child, unexpected separation and divorce, contemplation of suicide, and miscarriage—you will witness the powerful hand of God in helping these amazing women to rise after trial and tragedy just like the Phoenix rises from the ashes. As Minister Mary Harris so clearly expresses in her story following her unexpected three-year separation from her husband and ultimate divorce, "When you're in the dark you can't see the light, but you know the light is somewhere." Or in the words of Rhonda Bunch-Turner who lost her 21-year-old son in a tragic incident, "God will not give you more than you can bear." The extreme faith demonstrated in each co-author's story will have you on the edge of your seat as you envision what their experience was truly like and as their stories resonate deeply in your spirit, ignite the fire in your soul, and increase your faith in God.

Faith for Fiery Trials promises to touch you at your core as it reveals the human emotions we oftentimes experience when we're faced with life-altering trials including placing the blame on God, and what is required to surrender, release, and allow things to be done according to His will. As you immerse yourself in this book, you will discover that even the most difficult trials help us to develop godly character, and that enables us to rejoice in our tribulations, because we know that, "There's more to come: We continue to shout our praise even when we're hemmed in with troubles, because we know how troubles can develop passionate patience in us, and how that patience in turn forges the tempered steel of virtue, keeping us alert for whatever God will do next. In alert expectancy such as this, we're never left shortchanged. Quite the contrary—we can't round up enough containers to hold everything God generously pours into our lives through the Holy Spirit!" (Romans 5:3-5 MSG)

As you turn the pages of this book, prepare yourself to experience both the hurt and the healing of each story. Give yourself permission to sit in a space of meditation after reading this book to reflect on the love and grace that God has granted you through some of your most challenging trials. Then, praise His almighty name for the abundance of kindness and goodness that He has granted to you and each of the women in this book and work on increasing your faith in His promises. And don't ever forget where your strength to soar originates, "I can do all things through Christ who strengthens me." (Philippians 4:13 NKJV)

Cheryl Wood
International Motivational Speaker, Best-Selling Author & Professional Speaker Development Coach
www.CherylEmpowers.com

CONTENTS

Dedication v

Foreword vii

Introduction xiii

A Prescribed Fire 1

The Hand of God Guided Me Through the Fire 13

Faith, Fire and Fertility 23

Faith in a Fiery Furnace 33

Fuel Your Faith 45

Eradicating Rejection and Finding Your Beautiful 57

Tap into What's Already Inside of You 69

Strength from Within 81

There Should Have Been Four 93

Healing My Son and Me 103

Fear, Faith and Restoration: A Married Woman's Testimony 115

Cancer Was My Gift 127

Lessons Learned 137

Grieving in Truth 145

The Faith and Grace of a Warrior 159

Burnt but Blessed 171

Losing Erin 183

Conclusion 197

Meet the Co-Authors 199

Meet the Celebrity Authors 203
About the Visionary.. 207
Other Books by Elder Nicole S. Mason.................... 209

Introduction

Faith is like a muscle that needs to be developed. Life and the experiences that we endure serve as the tool to develop our faith. Everyone has faith. Romans 12:3 says, " . . . God has dealt to each one a measure of faith." (NKJV) Faith is belief—what we believe in, what we believe for and what we believe will be the outcome of a matter. Now, I admit from the onset of your time with me and the authors of this book that life is hard at pivotal points and at life-changing times. We all experience them, no one and I mean no one is exempt!

One of the pivotal points in my life that helped to develop my faith happened on June 7, 1992. I was a recent graduate of Howard University—29 days to be exact. I was sitting in the car with a friend and two men walked up to the car, opened fire and murdered my friend. As for me, this is the life-altering moment that I realized that there is a God, who is bigger than everything and everyone, and He saved me for a time such as this.

When the shots rang out that night, I remember vividly screaming, "*Jeeeeesssuuss.*" It seemed like I was hollering for a long time, but it was only a few minutes. It felt like things were moving in slow motion. I felt this overwhelming feeling like something picked me up out of the car, set me far enough down the street for me to "come to myself" and run as fast as I could. I don't remember opening the car door. I don't remember crossing the streets. When I "came to myself," I was approximately a block and half from where my car was parked. As I ran, I could hear the gunshots still ringing out behind me. I was trying to run to my sister's house about three blocks away.

I only ran a short distance, but in my mind, I thought I had been shot. My body began to respond to my thoughts. I couldn't run any further, because I was out of breath and panting heavily. I couldn't seem to catch my breath. My legs were weak, and I was just about to get down on my hands and knees to start crawling, when I looked up and saw two people sitting on a porch. I started hollering, "They shot him. They shot him." The man and woman didn't ask me any questions. They didn't want to know if anyone was following me or not. It was almost as if they were waiting for me. When I think about them now, and I can still see them vividly in my mind today. The woman resembles the lady who used to do the Pine Sol commercial. She was heavy set and had long dreadlocks. The man was short and had what I would describe as a perfect bush. There wasn't a hair out of place on his head. The shape of the bush was round and just that, perfect. They told me to come inside. The woman told me to lay down on the floor. I remember the room had lots of white in it—white curtains or blinds and a white lace mat on the floor (it reminded me of the lace doilies my grandmother used to have on her dresser). I don't remember if there was any furniture or not. The woman began to speak to me to tell me that everything was going to be just fine. The man called my sister and told her what happened and the address of the house. My sister picked me up, so that I could go back to tell the police that I was in the car.

When I arrived back at the scene, I talked to the first police officer I saw to tell him that was my car. They already had my purse with my identification, because it was in the car, along with the keys in the ignition. Unfortunately, the officer put me in a police cruiser that was parked right next to my car with the driver's side door open, and I could see my friend's dead body slumped over into the seat that I occupied not 15 – 20 minutes prior to that very moment. I totally lost it and had an uncontrollable melt down right there. The police whisked me away from the scene down to the police department headquarters and they questioned me until the sun rose. I was alone, scared, on edge and dazed to say the least.

Throughout this entire life-changing time in my life, God was showing me that He was there the whole time. It was during this time that I gave my heart to the Lord. The guy that was arrested for my friend's murder pled guilty saving me the anguish of having to testify. I began putting the pieces of my life back together but with a new normal. My level of faith had increased dramatically during this time. I was clear that God stepped out of Heaven to save me on that fateful morning at 1:30 a.m.

Life-changing events cause our faith to develop and increase. It changes our perspective on life from negative and unsure to positive and confident about what God can do and what He will do. It moves us from little trust to more trust in God. It sets the tone for our faith walk with God, and it allows us to serve as an example to others that God can be trusted, and He will show Himself merciful and gracious.

We use past events in our lives to help us get through events that will happen in the future. The

FAITH FOR FIERY TRIALS

event on June 7, 1992, and the details associated with it have developed my faith in a tremendous way. I'll end with this detail of my story. My mother and I were talking about two years after the event, and she just casually mentioned to me that she went back to thank the people who helped me that morning. I gave her the address. My sister confirmed that the address was correct, because she picked me up from the house and watched me come out of the house. My mom told me that she went back to the address about three days after the event to say thank you, but the person that answered the door told my mom that no one by the descriptions I gave her ever lived there.

I encountered angels that morning assigned to save my life. My faith in God is unshakeable, undeniable and unequivocal. I am confident that this book is going to develop faith for some, deepen faith for others and overall, enhance your relationship with God and ignite a blazing fire in your soul!

Elder Nicole

Nicole S. Mason, Esquire
Washington, DC

PASTOR JOYCE GILMER

A Prescribed Fire

Often, the earliest messages we receive in life are the ones that stick with us for the rest of our lives. This holds true for me with the indelible lessons etched in my mind regarding fire. Those earlier periods of instruction were to recognize fire to be extremely hot, harmful and as an agent that most assuredly could cause great pain. It didn't matter if it were a tiny spark ignited as a result of the friction wheel, turned by the thumb on a butane lighter, a flame generated from the pilot light on the gas stove, or a raging wildfire in California triggered by some careless passerby. Fire has been characterized and proven to be destructive and relentlessly uncontrollable once it has been set to take course.

I must admit, even as an adult, the dancing orange and red flames and intense heat emission, can still create some pause and trepidation. My traditional childrearing in a fairly religious environment reinforced that frame of thought, with fire and brimstone messages about hell. If there is anything that can confirm a negative connotation about fire, it would be the depiction of hell being full of raging fire, ready to eternally burn sinners and disobedient saints. When I turn on the stove to cook a meal or light the fireplace on a cold night, I am still cautious, because of those early lessons and impressions. However, as I've grown in age, wisdom and in spiritual discernment, I've also come to discover that fire has benefits.

Not every encounter with natural fire destroys, disrupts and devastates. Fire is used to prepare wonderful family dinners and holiday meals, to warm cold homes in the winter and to roast marshmallows around a campfire. In fact, there are some natural forest fires that are intentionally set because of the ultimate positive environmental effects it will have on the forest. That is known as a Prescribed Fire. It is one that is planned and controlled, in order to get rid of the dead trees, diseased vegetation and insects that are causing stagnation and harm to the ecosystem. Prescribed fires are an indication that there are healthy forests that have dead trees and plants that can decay and delay future growth. However, when a fire is prescribed, its path is controlled, and it's not released to annihilate everything. It's strategically aligned to burn up that which has been identified as unhealthy, damaging and dead. Once those things are burned to the ground, their ashes actually become nutrients to the soil and it causes regeneration, revitalization and renewal for the forest.

The Prescribed Fire

From a spiritual perspective, I am convinced that there are times in our lives when God assigns a prescribed fire for us to go through. It is a trial or test that is undeniably difficult and may seem out of our control, yet it is designed by God to increase our faith, burn away dead things, bring glory to His name and to usher us into a renewed place in Him. We must always remember that no matter how out of our control a situation or circumstance may appear, it is always in His control. As believers and Christians, there is nothing that happens to us that God doesn't allow and that He ultimately cannot lead us through or bring us out of. Although we will have ultimate victory, it's necessary to understand at this juncture that the prescribed fire may bring confrontation and consequences to challenge your faith. But, just as the prescribed fire is not intended to destroy the entire natural forest, it's not intended to destroy you.

Instead, we must assess our disposition and take pause to determine the lessons of faith, persistence, pruning, maturity, strengthening and even promotion, that God may be trying to walk us through, for His glory and our victory.

To further illustrate this concept of the prescribed fire, let's review the Biblical narrative of the three Hebrew boys, Shadrach, Meshach and Abednego, found in Daniel, chapter 3 and hone in on a few key points. The backdrop of this account reveals to us that the king made a golden image 90 ft tall and 9 ft wide and erected it in the Babylonian province. He summons those who held high office to the dedication of the statue, including the three Hebrew boys, who also had high ranking positions working for the king. During the ceremony, all people were commanded to follow King Nebuchadnezzar's orders to bow down and worship the golden image he set up, as soon as they heard the sound of the musical instruments play. Those who refused to bow would suffer the consequence of being thrown into the blazing fiery furnace. When all the people heard the flute, harp, sackbut, psaltery, dulcimer and other instruments play, they fell down and worshipped as the king had commanded. Well, everyone that is, except Shadrach, Meshach and Abednego.

FAITH FOR FIERY TRIALS

When the king questioned their disobedience to his orders, he reminds them what will happen if they do not worship his god and he mockingly poses the question, "Who is that God that shall deliver you out of my hands?" It's in that moment of confrontation that the Hebrew boys speak up. They do not stutter, stammer or hesitate to stand strong in their faith and decree that the God they serve is able to deliver them from the fiery furnace and out of the hand of the king. When you are confronted by devastating situations, does your faith cause you to speak, does it cause you to act or does it cause you to be silent? These boys were being threatened with literal fire, by a hostile force that had the power to make good on his promise. Yet, they had unshakeable faith and a willingness to deal with the consequences. They were not going to give in and bow down to any false god, when they knew they were serving the true and living God.

How strong are you in your faith? What will you do when you receive the doctor's report, or a notice of foreclosure or eviction? How will you endure traumatic marital problems or loss of a loved one or job? These are examples of modern day fires that may come to try your faith, make you want to back down and give in to the fear, depression, feelings of hopelessness, or make you want to tap into that inner hustler to handle things on your own. Living the God-kind of life requires us to dig our heels deep into the ground when we may want to tuck-tail and run. However, when you make a conscious decision to stand in faith, there will be consequences and conflict. When the three Hebrew boys spoke up, the king commanded for the fire to be turned up seven times hotter. The fire was so hot that it killed the strong men, who tied and bound the Hebrew boys and cast them fully clothed, into the furnace. This is a great place to shout! I prophesy to you and say, if you choose to stand fast in your faith in the midst of what you are dealing with, the enemy assigned to destroy you, will himself, be destroyed.

You Will Not Be Burned

I speak over your life, that you will not be burned. You will deal with tragic situations, broken-heartedness, disappointments, or wounds that cut so deep; you'll want to give up. You will deal with sparks, flickers and may even end up bound and in raging flames like the characters in the story, but you will not be burned. In fact, we have a guarantee in the Word of God for that. The latter portion of Isaiah 43:2 (NIV) says, "When you walk through the fire, you will not be burned. The flames will not set you ablaze." It doesn't say "if" you walk through, but "when" you walk through. In that one portion of text alone, we find the hard truth, that we will be placed in the fire, and rather than God rescuing us out of it, we'll be forced to walk through it. But we also have the overwhelming reassurance that when it's all said and done, we will not be destroyed. That's powerful! So many times we just want out of situations, but when God has us in a prescribed fire, it's often because He wants to keep us there, so He can manifest His presence and power by stepping into the flames with us.

Later in the narrative, King Nebuchadnezzar looks up and sees four men loose and walking in the midst of the fire. We believe the only way to be free is to avoid it all together or to get out, but God is saying when you exercise faith outside the furnace, I'll make you a firewalker when you get in the furnace. We're looking for rescue from it, while He's saying I'll make you free in the midst of it. God will render the fire powerless, take the heat out of the flames, make sure that what was supposed to kill you ends up being destroyed and you will not be burned!

Some of the most famed victory nuggets often highlighted from this story, in addition to their bodies not being burned, is that their hair wasn't singed, their garments didn't catch fire and they didn't smell like smoke. How in the world are you bound up and cast into a blazing fire and come out with that level of victory?

I submit to you that it all started with a determined faith in God and willingness to defy the king. Who or what are the kings you need to defy in your own life? When you take that kind of stand to exercise faith during fiery trials, you will walk out with the power that changes hearts, reverses decisions, rectifies wrong actions, causes promotions and releases the hand of God to bless you with an undeniable victory. In the end, their defiance and faith cause the king to change his word, bless the God he mocked them for serving, and he promoted them!

My Moment in the Flame

The longer you walk with God, the more aspects of His deity you begin to experience and the more opportunities you have to exercise your faith in the midst of trying times. One Wednesday evening, my husband calmly walked into the room to tell me he was feeling numbness and tingling in his leg and arm and needed me to take him to the hospital. What started off as a visit to the ER turned into tons of tests and a three-day stay in the hospital, with no real diagnosis, although they initially suspected a heart attack or slight stroke, which by the way, I was rebuking immediately. With the inconclusive findings, the neurologist and cardiologist released him from the hospital Saturday afternoon and cleared him to fly for an important business trip he'd already scheduled to Chicago that Monday. He was due back Wednesday, so Tuesday evening after a meeting, I called to check on him. He sounded weak and not like himself at all. When I asked him what was wrong he told me he was in the ambulance heading to a hospital in Chicago. The immediate concern grew more intently into worry as he was now back in the hospital miles away, after being released just two days prior. I was home alone and prayed most of the night. While in prayer, I asked the Lord what my act of faith during the waiting period should be. I sensed very heavily the Lord responding and sharing that this experience was merely a smokescreen and we were dealing with the symptoms but not really the problem. I needed to defy and fall out of agreement with the worry and doubt that was trying to incite unrest in my spirit and emotions. I firmly believe that whatever you feed the longest is the strongest, and I needed to feed and activate my faith and that is what I did.

I set the intention to pray strategically, but not for my situation or myself, but for others. So, Wednesday morning although I was still unsure of what was going on with my husband in Chicago, I established an all-day prayer watch. I went online and shared with my social media followers I was going into prayer that day and to send me any requests. No one except for my pastors and close family knew what I was going through. I ended up with 128 names and situations. I created a digital prayer wall and set the intention to pray three times that day at 9 a.m., 3 p.m. and 6 p.m. I earnestly prayed and called out every single name and situation asking God to move on behalf on His people. What I discovered was that while I believed and prayed for others in the midst of my own trial, God was moving in Chicago for us. He was lifting the smokescreen, clarifying answers and making sure my husband made his flight to get back home that night.

When he returned and went back to the original team of doctors, a proper diagnosis was made. Although he was placed on a heart monitor and needed surgery for something completely unrelated to the heart, it was a definitive fix, instead of the perpetual threat of a heart attack. And unless we shared it, you wouldn't know he couldn't speak above a whisper for three months after surgery, but he still got a promotion while he was in recovery! I'm still trying to figure out how God did that when he couldn't even go in to work. Today, he's committed to his daily two-hour workouts at the gym and preparing to run the annual 6.2-mile race in our state, the same way he's always done. There is literally no sign of smoke. It's a perfect example of God getting in the flames with you and walking you through the fire. When you make the decision to stand in faith and voice activate the victory you want to see, there are some guaranteed wins attached to your life. Whenever you are in a fire prescribed by God, you will emerge renewed, revitalized and refreshed. You will always gain the victory, and God will always get the glory.

RHONDA BUNCH-TURNER

The Hand of God Guided Me Through the Fire

Isaiah 43:2 (NLT) *" . . . When you walk through the fire of oppression, you will not be burned up; the flames will not consume you."*

1 Peter 1:7 (NLT) *"These trials will show that your faith is genuine. It is being tested as fire tests and purifies gold . . . "*

On August 6, 2011, I walked through fire unscathed and I had to exercise faith in God that I wasn't even aware that I had. In the early morning hours around 2:15 a.m. I received a phone call that changed my life forever. All weeklong leading up to that day I had a heavy darkness on my spirit that I couldn't even pray away. When I prayed, the feeling got lighter, but it never completely left me.

I was at my second job when I received a phone call from my son's godmother saying that a doctor at

NICOLE S. MASON, ESQUIRE

Fort Washington Hospital was trying to contact me regarding my son, Elijah. Before she could tell me why, a second call was coming into my cell from a 301-292 exchange, a Fort Washington phone number. I clicked over to Elijah's godbrother telling me that Elijah had been jumped and he wasn't responding to the doctors. I don't remember everything else that was said, but what stands out vividly in my mind every time I think about that night is a male doctor in the background yelling, "Is that his mom?" His godbrother replied, "Yes." The male doctor yelled, "Tell her to get here now!"

From the moment his godmother called me, I was extremely calm. This was very odd because I've never been calm whenever my children are or have been hurt. It was a peace that I could not explain, and I don't believe I had ever felt that sense of peace until that night.

I was 30 – 40 minutes away from Fort Washington while my son was laying there unresponsive. It was the wee hours of the morning and I wasn't driving. I prayed to God asking him to let me get to my son.

Elijah usually dropped me off or picked me up in his dad's car. Neither of us had our own car at the time, which is why I was working two full-time jobs. He had just completed 1,500 hours to become a barber. (I accepted his diploma posthumously.) Also, he had just passed the real estate exam for Washington, DC. I had introduced him to a good friend and her husband. They are brokers and the husband was so impressed with Elijah. He said Elijah reminded him of himself at that age. He took Elijah under his wing as his protégée, but they never got the chance to work together. Elijah had big goals and didn't want to work for anybody but himself. As soon as he told me that he needed a reliable car and a laptop, I got a second job. A job that I got in about three days because Elijah had referred me to the supervisor who showed up at that very moment while I was deep in thought about my son. The hand of God!

My supervisor said he was coming to check on me to see how things were going. I had been on the job maybe a month. I told him about the phone call I had just received. He said, "Oh no, you have to go. Let me go check on the guy in the other building and I will be right back to find someone to cover your post. But if you have to leave before I get back, I understand. I'm praying for you and your son. Your job will be fine. Just keep me posted on what's going on."

As I stood outside and waited for Elijah's godmother or a cab to arrive, I looked up to the sky and noticed there were many more stars than usual shining in the night sky. I remember saying, "God I don't know what is going on, but I pray Your will be done. I trust

You." I noticed a small opening in the sky with a white light shining through along with beams of white lights gliding over the sky. As I stood there, it felt as if someone was pouring relaxing hot oil on top of my head and it dripped down my entire body to my feet. That peace that I had felt moments earlier had returned but it was magnified. I noticed the heaviness that was in my spirit was completely gone, and I knew in my heart that my son had passed on from this side of heaven.

I noticed that there were no cars on the streets or people on the sidewalks this particular night. It was rather strange because during my time there the previous Saturday mornings in the wee hours, I noticed people leaving the various bars and restaurants that aligned the street. It was a beautiful summer night. My thoughts were interrupted by headlights. It was a cab. I flagged him and told him where I needed to go. He was hesitant at first. But he said it would cost $40. I told him I would pay $100.

As I sat in the back of the cab, I was amazed at how calm I was and how much of a peaceful state I was in knowing what I knew. Any other time I would have been out of my mind, but this time was different. It was as if I almost didn't recognize myself. I saw a meter in the cab. Oddly, the driver turned it off. The cabbie asked me if I worked there and if that was why it was urgent that I get there. I told him that my son had been involved in something and he was unresponsive. He was quiet for a while. Then he said, "I'm so sorry. No matter what your son will be fine." We rode the rest of the way in silence. Once we pulled up to the hospital, he said sadly, "I feel bad. I don't want to charge you. It's okay, go see about your son." I handed him $100 and didn't allow him to refuse it. He said, "You are a special lady. You, my friend, are going to be okay."

Many times, I thought back to that night with a myriad of questions. Why was he driving on that street on that night? What made him turn the meter off? Why did he emphasize "You are going to be okay?" Once during my reflections and questions, I was led to Hebrews 13:2 that says, *"Don't forget to show hospitality to strangers, for some who have done this have entertained angels without realizing it."* (NLT) God said it and I believe it. That cab driver was an angel that night who was assigned to me. The hand of God!

As I calmly walked through the hospital doors, I noticed the countenance on the faces of the entire medical staff fell when I said I was Elijah Turner's mom. I know they are trained to remain neutral, but I saw through their expressions. A doctor came over and said Elijah had been attacked by a group of guys and he wasn't responding. They were airlifting him to Washington Hospital Center (Medstar) because of the trauma to his head.

I noticed Elijah's godmother, godbrother, and cousin standing there when the doctor asked me if I wanted to see him. I said, "No. I will see him at Washington Hospital Center." A medivac nurse standing next to the stretcher that my baby was lying on said "Mom come over and kiss your son." I don't remember walking over, but there I was looking down at my child. He looked like he was sleeping. He looked like himself other than the cut under one of his eyes. But as I looked closer I saw someone's shoe print on my son's face. Amazingly, I was still peaceful and calm when I silently asked God, "Somebody stomped my child like this?" My child who just last week asked me for $10 to go buy himself some snacks but came back with only a Gatorade. When I asked what happened to his snacks he told me that the woman in front of him was short $9 on her order so he gave it to her and put his stuff back. My son who had been cutting the hair of elderly men that lived in our community, on a fixed income, for free for the last few months? My son who cuts the hair of little boys of single moms for free? My son who got up to let women, children, and elders sit down. As memories raced through my mind about how big my son's heart was, I couldn't believe God allowed him to meet this fate. Before I got too far into questioning God, that overwhelming sense of peace seemed to grip me tightly. It felt surreal as if I was being tightly hugged around my entire body with so much warmth.

I noticed a dried tear line down the right side of his face. As tears welled up in my eyes, it appeared as if the tear line on his face spelled "Mom." I was taken aback because my children call me Ma. I leaned down to kiss his cheek and whispered in his ear words that I never told anyone until this writing. I told him, *"I'm okay. We all will be fine if you want to go. Be free. Fly on son."* The tears gently flowed down my face as I watched the medivac nurse roll him to the helicopter.

My children's dad was already there when I arrived at Washington Hospital Center. He said the helicopter was landing as he pulled up, but he hadn't spoken to anyone yet. Lots of other family and friends started trickling in. Whenever I drive down Michigan Avenue, I always look up to that spot where my family and friends gathered. Around 6:00 a.m., Elijah's dad and I met with one of the doctors. She stated in her medical opinion that Elijah was brain dead due to the blow he took to the back of his head. She went on to say, "But things can change. I don't know if you are religious or not, but miracles happen." I think she asked our religion. At this point Elijah (the father, yes our oldest son was his namesake) stormed out. I reached for his arm and told him to just listen to her. He snatched his arm away from me. It was then we saw our son being rolled past us to the intensive care unit. That was the first time that Big Elijah had seen Lil' Elijah since everything had taken place. I will never forget the look on his face. At that moment, I knew that he knew what I had already known in my heart. He walked off.

I continued talking to the doctor and she explained that the only way to be 100% sure was to perform a cerebral angiogram, a test that would detect brain activity. That test wasn't performed until two days later on Monday, August 8, 2011. When I speak of the day my son passed, I always say August 6, 2011, because I already knew shortly after it happened that it was only his shell in the hospital that weekend hooked up to those machines. His death certificate reads August 8, 2011, at 10:30 am because that was the time the test results came back that there was no brain activity.

Even though I knew in my heart what the cerebral angiogram proved, another confirmation occurred later in the day on August 6th. There were lots of loved ones with me in the family waiting room. My little cousin, who was maybe four at the time, was standing on the threshold between the waiting room and the hallway. Actually, he was standing more in the hallway. His mom, my cousin, was seated next to me. She told him to come over with us to be closer to us so he wouldn't be by himself. He said, "I'm not by myself. Elijah is right here with me."

I don't like the way Elijah's life ended, and I tell God that whenever I think about what happened to him that night. But I chose long ago not to dwell on the events of that night. I choose to thank God for the 21 years I had with my son. I choose to thank God for all the lives my son touched. And there were many. I already knew my son was special and had a big heart, but the stories I learned about him after his passing made me that much prouder to be his mom, his Ma. I choose to remember that he was never truly mine to begin with. I was the vessel that God used to bring him into this world. He was only on loan to me. I choose to thank God for the love he had for all his family and me. I choose to thank God that Elijah's transition taught me that life is too short, and we don't know when our time is up. More importantly, I thank God for the strength and courage to put one foot in front of the other every day and enjoy this journey called life after surviving the unimaginable task of burying my child.

If I can encourage anyone it would be to willfully, purposely, intently choose each day to be joyful. Living life without a loved one hurts, but you can still smile when you think of something funny they said or did. Thank God for the memories and build new memories. Don't rob the loved ones that are still here by checking out on them mentally. Life will get hard at times. Trials will continue to come. Time does not heal the wound of a loved one passing, but if you learn the true value of time it will teach you to adjust to life, so you can finish your assignment and love on the family and friends who are still with you while remembering and honoring the ones who went on to Paradise ahead of you. You will learn to live your life without their physical presence because you will always carry them in your heart, your mind, and your spirit. God is amazing, and He is true to His Word. He truly will not give you more than you can bear. No matter your cross, you too can walk through the fire unscathed while hurting, crying, rejoicing, praising and praying while holding on to the hand of God.

CHARLOTTE E. AVERY

Faith, Fire and Fertility

I remember the day I found out I was pregnant. I was so overwhelmed because we had just moved to California. I really could not believe that God would allow me to be pregnant at such an awkward time in my life. My husband was so happy and excited to be a dad for the third time. Our older two children were too young to know they had a new sibling coming. After a little time had passed, we told some of our new neighbor friends. That November, my mom came to visit for my birthday; we told her the news, and, boy, was she surprised.

For weeks, I felt and watched my body change and grow. At my first doctor's appointment, I heard our baby's heartbeat. The doctor said our baby was growing and had a strong heartbeat. I felt like I could breathe a little easier.

NICOLE S. MASON, ESQUIRE

That December, our family of four and a half hopped on a plane to go home to Virginia for the holidays. I was so excited; we would get to see our family and friends and tell them we had another baby on the way. Little did I know that I would be leaving California with a baby in my womb and returning without one.

After being in Virginia for a few days, we drove to North Carolina to visit my husband's family. Our daughter was not yet a year old, but while we were there, we celebrated my son turning two. When we returned to Virginia, all things seemed well. On New Year's Eve I woke up feeling fine. As the day went on, I noticed that I was spotting. I called my doctors in Virginia. They did not seem alarmed, but they told me to come to the ER just to make sure all things were well. They said I may simply need to rest.

The wait in the waiting room seemed like forever. Finally, the nurse called me. As the technician ran tests, I knew something was wrong. The technician barely said a word to me. When everything was done, my favorite doctor came into the hospital room and gave me the most difficult news I could ever hear. She told me that although I was thirteen weeks pregnant, our baby was measuring small and there was no heartbeat. I was in a daze as I heard the words she spoke. How could this be possible? What did I do wrong? Why did this happen? Was this really happening to me, and on New Year's Eve? I was stunned. In less than twenty-four hours my hopes and dreams had been shattered.

During that moment, everything seemed to be moving so fast. My doctor said that it was in the best interest of my health for her to schedule an emergency procedure for them to take the baby. I remember my husband praying with the doctors and then falling asleep. Hours later I woke up crying desperately, "My baby, I want my baby." But there was nothing. Our baby was gone. When the doctor came in to see me, my husband asked the doctor what she thought happened. She sympathetically responded, "We don't know what went wrong. He was not growing." That is when I knew my baby was a boy.

There are no words to express how devastated I was. I was miserable. I did not want to leave the hospital. I just wanted to stay there one night so I could at least get myself together before returning to my mom's house, seeing the faces of my little ones, and breaking the heart wrenching news to anyone that might be there. I didn't want to hear anyone's voice or see anyone's face. I just wanted my son back.

When we got to my mom's house I went upstairs to sleep. I woke up the next morning crying and wanting my baby back. I stayed in bed for hours. When I finally got up, I went and looked at myself in the bathroom mirror. My body, the home of my baby was empty. I just stood there and cried. I just couldn't and didn't want to believe that my baby was gone. I even bought a pregnancy test hoping and praying that it would be positive, that all of this was just a bad dream. Clearly, God would not allow me to go into the New Year like this.

To make matters worse, a few days after all of this heartbreak, I had to get on a plane, leave my familiar place, and go back to California. Just the thought of going back there was terrible. I did not want to be there, and I also did not want to have to explain to our new friends what had happened. I left Virginia sad, empty, and very broken.

I had been through some fiery circumstances in my life, but the burn of this situation was like none other. No one really knew the depth of my heartbreak or the plight of my pain, not even my husband. I didn't understand or know what he was feeling either. Honestly, I was slightly perturbed that he didn't tell me what he was feeling. He really wanted me to be okay, and he did his best. But inside I was a miserable, broken mess and the fire kept burning.

I felt cheated out of my process to deal with and grieve the loss of our baby. When I got back to California, I had to be a wife and a mommy. I never felt like time stopped long enough for me to really vent and deal with the deep pain of losing my baby, my son. I was silently mad, hurt, and angry. I was mad because I was in California, and I was mad at God for taking our baby from us. I knew God was sovereign, but it didn't make losing my baby any easier.

Two months after my miscarriage, God used the least likely person to give me an opportunity to regurgitate all my anger, hurt, pain, frustration, rage, and disappointment. Through this person, I was able to deal with the raw and very real feelings that I had stuffed away. In one God ordained phone call, I was given the time and space to scream, cry, cuss, and vent without any judgment. She was 3,000 miles away, but she felt my heart and prayed for me. It was in that moment, I was able to find peace. I was no longer mad at God.

A few weeks later, while I was sitting in church, I heard the voice of the Lord ask me, "Is it well?" I said, "Yes, Lord it is well." Then, I remembered Philippians 4:7 that says, "And the *peace* of God, which surpasses all understanding, will guard your hearts and minds through Christ Jesus." (NKJV)

I didn't understand why I had a miscarriage, but I knew that God would give me peace and that His grace would be sufficient. And even though I didn't know when and I didn't know how, I had faith in knowing that God would birth something great through my pain. That was the day my joy began to blossom again.

While I had faith in knowing that God would birth a promise through my pain, I had no idea that about a month and a half later, I would find myself pregnant again. I was nervous and thrilled. I was thrilled that I was having a baby but being pregnant after losing a baby caused me to be on edge. Up until that point, I did not know if God would allow me to have any more children, but He did! Not only did God bless me with our daughter, He blessed me to birth four more children after her. That is right! I am the mom of seven of the most handsome and beautiful and wonderful people ever.

It was after the birth of my fifth child that I discovered God had given me the gift of fertility. Women who had a burning desire to be mothers started coming into my life. Some of them were newly married, some had been trying for years, and others had experienced multiple miscarriages. I would have dreams about women who wanted to have children. I would be out in various places with or without my children and people would ask me to pray for a friend, family member, neighbor, or coworker who wanted to have a baby. I could feel the longing in their hearts. Their pain, despair, loss and uncertainty were all too familiar. I was like, "Okay Lord, what do you want me to do with these women?" He told me that He wanted me to join my faith with theirs and share my gift of fertility with them. Talk about a *wow* moment.

One of the first times I shared my gift of fertility was when I was pregnant with my sixth child. A woman came to me and said, "You are such a beautiful pregnant mommy. You look so happy; this must be your first child." You can imagine how floored she was when I told her it was my sixth. That is when she shared her heart with me about wanting to have a baby.

I said, "Ma'am, you don't know me, but God has given me the gift of fertility. Can I pray for you?" With her permission, I prayed for her. My belly touched her; and as I prayed for her, my baby started moving. She was shocked. She cried, and I cried. I told her that she may never see me again, but I believed that God would give her the desire of her heart and that she would be a mother. Then I asked her for her first name, and I wrote it on a piece of paper. That is when the *Pregnancy Prayer List* began.

Another time, a good friend of mine called and told me about a friend of hers who was having difficulty having a baby. She asked if I would pray and believe that God would allow her friend to have a baby. We joined our faith and prayed for her friend. I asked God to allow my gift of fertility to flow to her friend. Less than six months later, I got a phone call saying that her friend was having a baby. Over the course of a year, God allowed me to pray for women who longed to have children and within a year or less these women were pregnant. Not long after that, I had a running list of women who wanted to be mothers. Some of these women didn't even know they were on the list.

On another occasion, I had a dream that our good friend and his wife were going to have a baby. Months before, I had an ache in my heart for them. It was the same ache that I had when I lost my son. The dream that I had was very vivid. In my dream I could touch his wife and feel the baby in her womb. I held him, smelled the sweet newborn smell that babies have, and I felt his skin on my cheek. It was so strong that I picked up the phone and called them. I told them my dream, and I said that I believed that they were going to have a baby. I told them that I was praying for my gift of fertility to flow through his wife. Almost six months passed when I called to see if we could schedule some time together. That is when he said, "Remember the dream that you told us you had? Well, we are having a baby boy." I screamed through the phone. Then he said, "Charlotte, God has truly given you a gift."

One day, God placed it on my heart to share how He had given me the gift of fertility to my social

FAITH FOR FIERY TRIALS

media community. He told me that there were people who needed me to share my gift with them. After I shared my post, my inbox filled up with requests of women who were my "friends" on social media and some who were friends of friends who wanted to be added to the *Pregnancy Prayer List*. That same year, five women on the list conceived. It was so beautiful and amazing. One of the women who sent me a request was a mom from my son's martial arts school. Her request was for a friend who was struggling to have another baby. Four months after putting her friend on the *Pregnancy Prayer List*, she in-boxed me to say that her friend was expecting. Because of her age and previous complications, her friend was categorized as having a high-risk pregnancy. Every time she went to the doctor to see the baby, my friend would send me a picture of the baby. Her friend had no idea that she had put her on the *Pregnancy Prayer List*.

When the baby arrived, my friend sent me a message that said, "Charlotte, they finally had the baby!" I was so happy for them. Then she said, "They had a baby girl. Guess what they named her?" I said, "What?" In the next breath, she said the words that blew me away, "They named her Charlotte!" She said, "My friends don't know you, and they named their baby girl after you! Charlotte, I think God used that to solidify in your heart and in your mind that He has truly given you a gift of faith and fertility." Talk about a *holy cow* moment. I am telling you, I was so taken aback, I cried in awe of God. Only God could do something that awesome.

It has been a little over 12 years since I lost my son, Nathaniel, through miscarriage. By the way, Nathaniel means given of God. And even though I didn't have him for long, there is no doubt in my mind that he was given and taken for a reason that is far bigger than I can understand. Had I not gone through the fiery trial of a miscarriage, I may not have the faith to stand in the gap for women who want to be moms.

Today, even as I write this, the *Pregnancy Prayer List* continues to grow. It now includes women who want to birth children physically and women who want to adopt children who have been birthed in their hearts. I count it an honor and privilege to join my faith, share my gift of fertility, and pray for every woman who is currently on or will be placed on the list. I thank you God for bringing me through fire that increased my faith and gave me the gift of fertility.

DR. MARY J. HUNTLEY

Faith in a Fiery Furnace

Have you ever faced what seemed to have been an unsurmountable challenge? Yes, you prayed the Prayer of Binding and Loosing, put God in remembrance of His Word according to Jeremiah 1:12, pled the blood of Jesus over the situation, but the mountain seemed to stand still, or in some instances became larger and refused to move. Maybe you resorted to fasting in conjunction with prayer. However, the situation continued to prevail. I feel strongly that we all have had our challenges with stubborn situations. However, we prevailed in the end because God cannot lie according to Numbers 23:19. Therefore, He showed up and delivered in the midst of our fiery furnace allowing us to proclaim victory.

On January 17, 1989, I faced a fiery furnace when I visited my primary care physician. A sonogram revealed an enlarged fibroid uterus. The sonogram also revealed that my right ovary was normal, but the left ovary and left kidney were not even visible as a result of a pelvic mass. Of course, the physicians immediately began to talk about emergency surgery. However, what they failed to realize was the fact that I had met with my Commander-in-Chief in my Spiritual Situation Room where I prayed and made my requests known before my doctor's appointment. I also anointed myself with oil, prayed the Prayer of Faith, pled and applied the blood of Jesus over my life and spoke healing scriptures daily. Therefore, I did not become alarmed when I heard my doctor's discussion regarding my possibility of undergoing emergency surgery. I knew that my heart faith in God would prevail in this fiery furnace. I recalled that Jehovah-Rapha, my healer, was still in charge, and that He had taken 39 stripes at Calvary to remedy *every* situation, *every* circumstance and *every* condition that would ever try to encroach upon my territory. Therefore, I continued to work full time as I exercised faith in God's Word for my healing.

Have you ever prayed consistently about a specific issue or concern? It may have even seemed as if the more you prayed, the hotter your fiery furnace became. Rest assured that you are not alone. Many times our faith is tested to allow us to see what kind of fruit we are producing. We must ask the question: "Are we patient enough?" God does not always answer our prayers in the manner that we think He will. Therefore, we should be patient. Let me remind you that the answer to Daniel's prayer was delayed for 21 days. In fact, God's Word says in Daniel 10:12-13, "Do not fear, Daniel, for from the first day that you set your heart to understand, and to humble yourself before your God, your words were heard; and I have come because of your words. But the prince of the kingdom of Persia withstood me twenty-one days; and behold, Michael, one of the chief princes, came to help me. . ." (NKJV) Just know that delayed is not denied and remember that heart faith will always prevail in the fiery furnace. Be encouraged because the first time you prayed God's Word and not the problem, He heard you. God doesn't have amnesia, He will not forget you. Surely, God is a rewarder of those who diligently seek Him.

Of course, while awaiting God's healing, noisome pestilences attempted to encroach upon my territory. However, I continued to remember that I was in a spiritual battle. I dressed myself in the whole armor of God and continued to trust Him. During the waiting period, my uterus continued to grow because of the pelvic mass. In all of this, I never experienced pain. I never missed time at work. God is so faithful! Finally,

I decided to get a second opinion about the matter. In November 1990, upon examination, the tumors had grown rapidly, and my doctor stated that I was susceptible to cancer. In fact, he was very concerned and alarmed about the size of my uterus and stated that I should not return to his office until I was ready to schedule surgery.

My heart faith was tested in the fiery furnace and the noisome pestilence became louder. However, I knew the difference between "head faith" and "heart faith." I continued to exercise heart faith. Head faith said, "I had waited long enough, and I know that it is not worth it." Heart faith said, "He that promised is faithful, and I received when I prayed." Head faith said, "This is ridiculous and makes no sense so why bother?" Heart faith said, "God places His Word over His name, so He has to make good on His promise." It was heart faith that caused the Syrophenician woman to hold on to Jesus when, ". . . He answered her not a word. His disciples came and urged Him, saying, 'Send her away, for she cries out after us.'" It was heart faith that would not be discouraged, even when Jesus told her that He was not sent to her. (See Matthew 15:23-28) *Heart faith is not easily deterred.* Head faith reasons with facts, logic and the noisome pestilences and becomes easily discouraged. *Deep down in my heart I knew that God would not fail me.*

FAITH FOR FIERY TRIALS

Finally, I consented to surgery after enduring the pelvic pressure of the mass. I discovered that one of the tumors was the size of a five-pound infant. However, God kept me in the midst of this fiery furnace and allowed me to prevail without smelling like smoke. Though I was challenged, I had a plan and exercised faith in God.

On January 15, 1991, I entered the hospital. Upon arrival, I remained focused on Jehovah-Rapha, my healer, fully confident in *His* ability. On the way to the operating room I reiterated to my husband "Stand on the Word of God and His promises." Once in the operating room, there were three primary care physicians present. First and foremost, Jehovah-Jireh was there, my attending physician/primary care physician was there, and unbeknownst to me, an oncologist was also present. The oncologist was scheduled because the five-pound tumor had grown quickly. No worries because nothing catches God by surprise. He was well aware of the situation and had it all in control. God was also aware of the fact that I had continued to trust Him and put Him in remembrance of His Word. When I awakened from the anesthesia, my doctor greeted me with the news that the tumors were benign (non-cancerous). My husband and I thanked God for that awesome praise report. Until the time of my primary care physician's death, I held the record for the largest fibroid tumor he had ever removed. *But God* was faithful. Yes, it was a very challenging time; my faith was under attack and noisome pestilences attempted to divert my attention in another direction. But my heart faith in Jehovah-Rapha prevailed. I could not allow anything to make me doubt the power of God. This I know; *God honors faith in His Word.* I held on to my faith.

My most recent fiery furnace occurred in November 2015, when I had another health challenge that tried to encroach upon my territory. I went for my regularly scheduled mammogram. My results showed that I had an abnormal reading. According to the doctors, I needed to return to have a follow up mammogram *and* a sonogram. Of course, I scheduled the second mammogram which yielded the same results. In fact, the nurse was very concerned and brought my husband into the examination room to share the results. I recall very vividly sharing with her how *God* had taken care of me thus far, and that *He* was so very faithful. Regardless of the challenge, I know and am thoroughly convinced that Jehovah-Jireh and Jehovah-Rapha live. Next, I was scheduled for a biopsy. Wow, what a fiery furnace test.

Once again, I exercised my faith in *God.* I made another appointment with my breast specialist at a breast center. In the interim, I continued to pray and believe God. I reported for my appointment at the breast center with my previous results on a CD, along with other accompanying paperwork. The breast specialist administered a manual breast exam, read my CD from the previous radiology facility, and reviewed my accompanying paperwork. While she left me in the examination room, I focused on healing scriptures. After careful examination, the breast specialist stated that *I did not require a biopsy. Glory to God*! However, I was required to have quarterly 3-D mammograms and sonograms until a one-year period lapsed with consistently normal readings.

The noisome pestilences continued to rise up. But I continued to exercise faith in Jehovah-Rapha. Once again, I continued to anoint myself with oil, and my husband and I prayed God's Word and repeated healing scriptures. Finally, in December 2016, I received the all clear from my breast specialist. *I did not require surgery*. I am back to my regularly scheduled yearly mammogram. *To God be all the glory*! How awesome is that? What a mighty God!

What would have happened had I given up and thrown in the towel? Where would I be? I could have gone home and had a pity party during both health challenges. However, I chose to exercise my big, bad, bold faith in the fiery furnace. God delivered me and brought me through with honors, not even smelling like smoke. I chose to tell those health challenges about my God. Isn't that what happened in the fiery furnace? Shadrach, Meshach and Abednego exercised their faith in God. They knew that not only was God able, but GOD was and is well able. Our El-Shaddai, more than enough, all-sufficient God is more than enough. He is able to do exceedingly abundantly above all you and I are even able to think or imagine. (See Ephesians 3:20) Remember that God is no respecter of persons. (See Acts 10:34) Since He did it for me, He will do the same for you. And He honors faith in *His* word. He is obligated to show up where He sees faith in action.

I am reminded that many have been led to believe that you must have a ton of faith to believe God and receive His promises. However, Matthew 17:20 confirms the amount of faith that is needed to please God and receive his promises, ". . . Because of your unbelief; for assuredly, I say to you, if you have faith as a mustard seed, you will say to this mountain, 'Move from here to there,' and it will move; and nothing will be impossible for you." (NKJV) So regardless of what tries to encroach upon your territory, use your mustard seed faith and the name of Jesus to speak to your mountain and watch it move. It is impossible for any issue or concern to remain active once you utilize mustard seed faith in the name of Jesus. God's Word must accomplish its goal as stated in Isaiah 55:11, "So shall my Word be that goes forth from My mouth; It shall not return to Me void, But it shall accomplish what I please, And it shall prosper in the thing for which I sent it." (NKJV)

What mountains are challenging you today? Is it finances, health, accomplishing your goals? Don't magnify your mountain or your problem; magnify your *God*. Tell every challenge about the power of your *God*. Exercise your faith and watch God deliver. I remind you that the God I serve specializes in things that *seem* impossible. Notice I said "seem" impossible. Nothing is too hard for God! He is not a man that He should lie, and He keeps His promises. All you need is faith in His Word and perseverance. I encourage you to continue to speak God's Word to every mountain that challenges you in the fiery furnace. Eventually, manifestation will show up, because God is faithful.

So what posture should we maintain while awaiting answers to our prayers? Always maintain an attitude of gratitude. After you have made your request known, praise God for the answer. Thank Him for present confidence based on past experience. Thank Him for the many prayers He has answered in the past. Continue to tell God what His Word says because He is bound and obligated to His Word. He promised that heaven and earth would pass away before one jot or tittle of His Word failed. Psalm 138:2 reminds us, ". . . For You have magnified Your Word above all Your Name." (NKJV) He has answered our prayers before, and *He will* do it again. We should stand knowing that we can count it all joy knowing that every challenge that comes our way has passed God's "clearance or approval." In essence, nothing surprises or catches God off guard. He simply allows us to be tested. It is during the times of testing that our spiritual fruit, faith, and character are revealed. We should not attempt to lock our infinite God into our finite timetable. We must remember that He is sovereign. Therefore, He does not need our permission or approval to respond to our requests as it pleases Him. We should continue to speak God's Word knowing that we will have what we say according to Proverbs 18:21, which states that, "Death and life are in the power of the tongue . . ." (NKJV) Speak God's Word until you see it. Continue to call those things that you do not see into existence. Know your rights as an heir of God and a joint heir with the Lord Jesus Christ. We have the same rights and privileges, so do not settle for less.

Finally, even when we implement these principles it may seem as if our prayers will not be answered. However, we must not waver. Just like Abraham, we must not stagger at God's promises. *Regardless of the waiting period, regardless of the noisome pestilences, know that nothing and no thing is too hard for God.*

DEBBIE ANDREWS

Fuel Your Faith

"You have Stage 1 Ductal Carcinoma breast cancer in your right breast." This disease is a noninvasive condition in which abnormal cells are found in the lining of a breast duct, and the cells have not spread outside to other tissues in the breast, lymph nodes or the body. I am thankful that the cancer was detected in its early stages and could be treated effectively. Even though the diagnosis was stage 1, it was still difficult for me to fully understand all that I had heard.

In my subconscious, my thoughts were, "Why is this happening to me?" "Are you sure?" "Am I dreaming?" I exercise regularly and eat healthy meals. I've always been very consistent with my yearly mammograms and hearing the breast cancer diagnosis was difficult for me to understand. I received the cancer diagnosis while I was taking a class at Calvary Bible Institute. Not surprisingly, it was a class on prayer. God always has a way to prepare you for what's coming. He was equipping me for a faith walk.

Shortly after the diagnosis, my breast surgeon discussed the surgery and other procedures regarding my health and wellness.

And the journey began. One of my siblings famously says that, "Your life is under a microscope." Yes, God is watching how you handle adversity, and folks are watching you, too. In my valley experience, I wanted to exemplify a positive attitude and represent the God in me.

After I met with the doctor, the nurse practitioner suggested that I meet with the Chaplain for further consultation. I was hesitant to expose my heart and converse with a complete stranger. I'm literally in denial, shock, and disbelief. No matter what adversities we are experiencing, Jesus is continuously the center, and we should always be a beacon of light in times of difficulty.

The tears quickly emerged as I sat in the Chaplain's small, sweltering office. As I relinquished my emotions and accepted the cancer diagnosis, I felt a hot surge of power. During our conversation, we discussed my family history, especially my parents, both of whom were diagnosed with cancer many years ago and had transitioned to paradise. I began to wonder how my parents reacted when they received their cancer diagnosis.

The Chaplain shared her story as a two-time breast cancer survivor, which was comforting to me. Isaiah 40:29 which states, "God gives strength to the weary and increases the power of the weak" strengthened my faith." (NIV) I knew God was in the middle of my storm, and the battle was not mine, but the Lord's. Of course, I would survive cancer, too! After the meeting, my sister-in-Christ, who came with me as support prayed powerfully. We worshipped and praised our God. My spirit agreed with every word she spoke into the atmosphere. At the close of the prayer, my mind immediately was calm. I had the confidence, fully believing that everything would work out by faith and for my good. Yes, I was confident of this very thing, that He Who has begun a good work in me would perform it until the day of Jesus. (See Philippians 1:6)

On January 17, 2013, I underwent a lumpectomy as well as an Intra-Operative Radiation Therapy (IORT). The Intra-Operative Radiation Therapy was a historic moment because I was the first patient at Washington Hospital Center to have this procedure administered.

Several weeks following the post-surgery, an Oncotype test of the removed cancerous tumor was examined to test the cancer recurrence level. My test results indicated the cancer recurrence of 16 percent. Therefore, as a precaution, my Oncologist suggested that I receive four rounds of chemotherapy treatments to be administered every three weeks. Additionally, my physician stated, "It's possible an undetected cancer cell may have unsuspectingly floated in other parts of the body during the surgical procedure."

I immediately addressed my concerns with the Oncologist, particularly about hair loss and other significant side effects. I was uncertain about the chemotherapy drugs and hoping to bypass the treatment. Logically, my intellect was programmed to believe the media viewpoints regarding chemotherapy. In my moment of anxiety, I called my sister for advice. She was undergoing her own battle with Stage 4 breast cancer, and she encouraged me to move forth in faith with the chemotherapy treatment. On March 28, 2016, my dear sister received her wings and transitioned to paradise. Reverend Dianne Harrod fought a good battle of faith, and she finished her race with dignity.

Finally, I calmed my nerves and reenergized my faith muscles. We must exercise our faith! The dictionary defines faith as, "belief in, devotion to or trust in somebody or something, especially without logical proof." The Bible teaches us that the substance of faith is a devotion to God, a belief, a complete trust

FAITH FOR FIERY TRIALS

that God will protect you. For example, Job, a great man of faith, worshipped and praised God though he lost his land, livestock, and his sons and daughters. (See Job 1:13-19). No matter the storm, we must hold fast to our faith with the assurance that God will prevail in our circumstances.

Faith can be demonstrated in many ways. Many soldiers go to combat in faith, not fear because they are fully equipped and trained for battle. The same thing applies to us on the battlefield; we must stand on the Word of God, which is our solid rock. Satan has no authority over the Christian believer, because God has given us His Word to comfort us and the Holy Spirit to empower us to walk in faith.

Remember the story of the three Hebrew boys? King Nebuchadnezzar made a golden idol and commanded the people to bow down and worship the golden image he had erected. Whoever did not follow the command would be thrown into a burning fiery furnace (See Daniel 3:4-6). The three Hebrew boys, Shadrach, Meshach, and Abednego did not honor the king's request to idolize the golden image. They indicated that God would deliver them from the fiery furnace. That's faith, believing for victory in the outcome before witnessing the ultimate manifestation of God's glory. The King threw the boys in the furnace, which was heated seven times hotter than usual. The Hebrew boys were in the furnace, walking around. The king commanded the Hebrew boys to step out of the fiery furnace, and when Shadrach, Meshach, and Abednego stepped out, the king noticed no harm had come to them, their hair was not burned, and they didn't smell like smoke. Trials do not come in our lives to hold us in captivity, but to strengthen us so that we rely solely on our heavenly Father to see us through, by faith. Yes, there will be trouble on every side, but no matter the fire, continue to walk in faith.

Another aspect of faith is that it's critically important to surround yourself with positive people and avoid those who attempt to plant negative seeds. Several people offered their assistance, but they were pessimists strategically assigned to me from the devil, that roaring lion that comes to kill, steal and destroy. Some went so far as to ask unhelpful, nonproductive questions and comments like: "You didn't check your breasts?" "Are you afraid?" "Will you need time off from work for disability?" "The treatments and medications will make you sick" "My mother, father, sister, brother, and dog died from cancer." Lord have mercy! Folks words have no impact when you have power on the inside. It's the Holy Ghost power which resides in each of us to shame, shun and shut the enemy down. There is one who speaks like the piercings of a sword, But the tongue of the wise promotes health. (Proverbs 12:18 NKJV)

Living in my testimony, I have learned that the devil is a defeated foe, and "No weapon formed against [me] shall prosper, And every tongue which rises against you in judgment You shall condemn." (See Isaiah 54:17 NKJV) As the devil detonated his fiery darts, I reverted those fiery darts right back. Fear is never an option, but faith is. It is impossible to please God without *faith*! Satan will try to torment you by any means necessary, and he will use folks to bewilder you and throw you off course. Nevertheless, stay on course and connect to your Source. We are divinely connected to the "Good Shepard," "The Light of the World," "The Kings of Kings," "The Lord of Lords," "The Bread of life," and His name is Jesus Christ!

If a woman can touch the hem of Jesus' garment and be healed, surely Jesus can heal a tumor. Jesus healed a blind man, surely Jesus can eradicate a tumor. Jesus raised Lazarus from the dead; surely, there is nothing impossible for Him! Yes, I've been through the fiery furnace, but I did not burn!

Don't allow afflictions, distractions, persecutions, malice or fiery furnace experiences to hinder you from reaching your God-given destiny. Beloved, when you find yourself in a fiery furnace, speak truth to power. The omnipotent, omnipresent God who reigns supreme will never leave you nor forsake you.

As my journey continues, I maintain my integrity and declare what I believe, and I believe in divine and supernatural healing. Recently, my colleague stated that I consistently speak positive affirmations. I do, indeed. I must always open my mouth and declare what I believe, so my words can manifest, and bring hope to my situation. Words are not just merely sounds releasing from our vocal cords, but our words have power. The power of our words can equip us to be our best selves in times of adversity.

We are not exempt from trouble but don't allow your circumstances to have dominion over you. Take authority over your circumstances. You have power on the inside to use your God-given authority and claim it by faith. In addition to prayer, I declare and decree healing affirmations over my entire body. One of my favorite scriptures is Isaiah 53:5, which states, "But He *was* wounded for our transgressions, *He was* bruised for our iniquities; The chastisement for our peace was upon Him, And by His stripes, I am healed." (NKJV)

During my chemotherapy treatments and frequent doctor appointments, I maintained a steadfast and faithful demeanor, instead of wavering in despair, anguish, and hopelessness. My hair started to fall out immediately after the first round of chemotherapy. I discovered that wearing wigs in the hot summer months was challenging. I recalled waiting for the metro bus, and the temperature in D.C. forecasted to be 99 degrees. Suddenly, I felt a cool breeze manifested in the atmosphere. The Holy Spirit's presence was invigorating. I continued my daily commute to work and exercise regimen throughout my treatments.

During the initial Oncotype test, my recurrence level was 16 percent, after treatment, the recurrence level dropped to five percent. I was blessed to learn that through all examinations, that there were no longer signs of cancer. God turned my stumbling blocks into stepping stones! "Now to Him who is able to do exceedingly abundantly above all that we ask or think, according to the power that works in us, to Him be glory in the church by Christ Jesus to all generations, forever and ever. Amen. (Ephesians 3:20-21 NKJV)

To God be the Glory for the marvelous things He has done! I was fit for the fight! I am victorious! I am fearfully and wonderfully made! I am a warrior! My surgical scars personify strength, resilience, and determination. Always fight a good battle of faith and understand that you have the spirit of the living God within you. Although forces are aggressive and wicked, they do not have to take residence in our lives and defeat us. We have the Lord with us, and the armor of God is our protection. Therefore, stand in position, keep your breastplate intact, and never surrender.

My personal experience living with and beyond breast cancer has taught me that my heavenly Father is always readily available to aid me in the time of urgency, and there are no restrictions to His access. It is as simple as conversing with God in prayer, trusting His faithfulness, and having a spirit of expectancy. I encourage you to talk to God, no matter what the need, as He is our source and strength, a present help in the time of trouble. We always have open access as Paul reminds us in Ephesians 2:18, for through Him we both have access by one Spirit unto the Father.

Prayer: Spirit of the living God we come in Your presence to say thank You. We know that Your Word is truth and power. Father, we are lifting survivors to You in the name of Jesus that You would keep them in perfect peace, asking that You would supply all their needs according to Your riches and glory. Father God, give my sisters the faith and the courage knowing that we have peace with You through our Lord and Savior, Jesus Christ. Even in tribulation, we know that patience produces hope because the love of God is shed abroad in our hearts by the Holy Spirit which resides in each of us. Our bodies are the temple of the Holy Spirit, and we are healed from the crown of our heads to the soles of our feet.

FAITH FOR FIERY TRIALS

We're praying that every blood vessel and cell will function normally to its maximum capacity in the name of Jesus. Cancer will not return but be eradicated and thrown into the depths of hell. We rebuke the spirit of doubt, despair, and discouragement, and declare victory in the name of Jesus. Lord, we thank You for the caregivers, for their sacrifices and their steadfast commitments. Father, for our sisters who received their wings and resting in paradise, we will continue to hold those precious memories in our hearts. Thank You, Father, for Your grace and Your tender mercies. Thank You for being our Jehovah-Rapha and our Jehovah-Jireh in the name of Jesus, *Amen.*

Life is precious, particularly when you can bounce back from your valley experience. As a breast cancer survivor, I appreciate each moment in this earthly realm. I'm grateful each day that I open my eyes, as my Heavenly Father breathes new life in me daily, because His mercies are new every morning. I will continue my affirmations and declare daily, "*It is well with my soul.*"

MINISTER TANESHIA CURRY

Eradicating Rejection and Finding Your Beautiful

"How could they leave me? Why did that happen to me? Was I not good enough? Was I not pretty enough? Didn't I do everything they wanted me to? What's wrong with me? What did I do wrong? Why don't they like me? Why won't they accept me?" These, and so many other questions, we ask over and over again when we have experienced rejection. To reject someone or something is, "To refuse to accept, consider, submit to, take for some purpose, or use; to refuse to hear, receive, or admit." Rejection comes in many forms and affects us on varying levels.

Please allow me these next few moments to share some of my run-ins with rejection and how, when the dust settled, and the smoke cleared, I found myself still standing and moving forward. If I can do it, *so can you*!

When I saw him run up to *her* on the playground and kiss *her* on the cheek, it was at that moment that I began to despise my brown skin, black hair and brown eyes. I wanted white skin, blonde hair and blue eyes like *hers*, because that's what the boy who looked like me with brown skin, black hair, and brown eyes—without saying any words—said was pretty. Growing up as the only black female in my classes throughout elementary, junior high and high school was extremely difficult. Never getting those notes saying, "I like you, do you like me? Check the box: Yes or No," does something to a person's self-image. To think, someone who looked like me, but didn't want me caused a self-rejection that was unexplainable.

It all started in elementary school, there on that playground. Then at the age of 13, my father was killed in a head-on train collision and from there, things spiraled downhill very quickly for me. My father, being a Sergeant in the military, did not do the "hugging-and-saying-I-love-you" thing. Although I knew my father loved me, I longed to hear "I love you" from him and then one day, he was gone! No warning or no goodbye which meant my chances of hearing those words or receiving those hugs was gone too. This began the downward spiral and as the proverbial saying goes, I began "looking for love in all the wrong places."

Not long after my father's death, I gave away "my gift" of virginity. The guy from the playground finally gave me the time of day and allowed me to give him "my gift" (behind a Pizza Hut by the way), because I didn't know my value and worth. It certainly didn't mean to him what it meant to me because after "it" happened, he walked away; never looking back and what I thought would fill a void, only made it worse.

Then *finally* in the eleventh grade, a fine-looking black male showed up in my hometown of Altoona, Pennsylvania and guess who he wanted to talk to? Yes, you guessed it, *me*! Later I found out it was me and many others, but that's another conversation for another book. The signs were all there that he was not committed to me like I was to him and his intentions were misguided, but because I only wanted to be loved and accepted, I ignored every last one of them. Trying to change him and making him love me became an addiction for me. He became my drug of choice. If we were supposed to go on a date and he didn't show, I searched the city looking for him just like a drug-addict would look for their next hit.

NICOLE S. MASON, ESQUIRE

Off to college I went. Maryland bound and free from him and the unhealthy situation. I was starting a new life, or so I thought. You do know that the devil uses people and things to hold you in bondage. He knows that if you ever *really* get free, you will be a force to be reckoned with. (I had to interject that right there). I left him in Pennsylvania and then he moved to Maryland! What in the world? He called me, invited me to his home and because my need to be loved had not been dealt with, again, I bypassed the signs, hopped on the Peter Pan bus and off to his house I went. Like an addict, I went back to what was familiar.

During one of those trips, I became pregnant. Forced to go back home to Pennsylvania, the obsession for love became even greater. Six months into my pregnancy, I received word that the man whose child I was carrying would be having a child with someone else and to add insult to injury, he brought her to my hometown to celebrate! Talk about rejection! Those questions came flooding through my mind again. "How could he do that to *me*?" "Wasn't I good enough?" "Wasn't I pretty enough?" And, on and on.

Ten years later, a different type of man sought me out. He loved church, so did I. He loved music, so did I. We had many things in common and when he told my mother that he wanted to marry me, *score* . . . the search for love had ended! This had to be God! With our relationship rekindled after his divorce and my break up, we began our journey to what I thought would be everything I needed and wanted it to be. However, the face of familiarity found me again and there I was pregnant with my second child, but this time I knew it would be different. *This* time, I would be married. However, seven months pregnant, on the day of burying my beloved maternal grandmother, he proceeded to tell me that there was someone else. Time stood still, and the wind was knocked out of me. Those questions came rushing back again only this time they were louder and more painful than before, *"How could he do that to me?" "Wasn't I good enough?" "Wasn't I pretty enough?"* With this rejection came a deep depression coupled with suicidal thoughts and despair.

While penning this chapter, I was fortunate for the Holy Spirit to reveal to me that the spirit of rejection not only came to try (key word *try*) to destroy me, but it came to try to destroy my children even before they were birthed into the earth. You see, I had become so consumed with my own pain during both of my pregnancies that I was unable to form the maternal bond with my children thereby allowing the seed of rejection to take root in the fruit of my womb. Thank You, Holy Spirit, for this revelation because now I know to fight the devil on behalf of my children!

Here's a little reminder, the devil knows who to come after. If you are or have been under attack, let that be a sign to you of the greatness that is inside of you!

Now that we've shared a bit, the question remains, how do we eradicate rejection, especially when it's been rooted for so long and it has gone so deep? Let's examine this question.

I'd like to suggest that you begin with *positive self-talk*. One of the manifestations of the root of rejection that I experienced showed up when I offered ideas, suggestions or the like. It seemed that when I said something, people would minimize what I had to say and brush it off as not being of importance or value. I am convinced that because I internalized the aforementioned instances of rejection instead of releasing them, I didn't value myself. Others can sense those insecurities and will capitalize on your shortcomings and fears for their own personal gain. Now, this is not everyone, but society has taught us to step on and over others to feel important and to be on top. Whatever the case may be for you or whatever seems to be truth for you, starting today, begin to validate yourself!

How I began to eradicate rejection and started on the path to find my beautiful was to start looking myself in the mirror and telling myself that what I had to say had value and was important. I know that's an oxymoron for someone who had been called to preach! Even though I have been called to minister to others, I had to first minister to myself and build myself up which is an ongoing process. To you, I say, from this moment on, be intentional and continuously do like David did in 1 Samuel 30:6 and encourage *yourself*!

Additionally, to eradicate rejection and find your beautiful, it is important that you *get the help you need*, if you need it. Set your pride down and be willing to say, "I need help." If after you have spoken positively over yourself and it seems that those deep feelings of rejection continue to overshadow you, if you need to, seek professional help. I, myself, see a psychologist and I love it! It has been the most freeing experience for me. It has taken me up a path to a healing that I wish I would have experienced a long time ago.

My psychologist listens to my deepest hurts, fears, concerns, or whatever I choose to share and offers information to help me process things from a different perspective while offering tools for continued growth, healing and personal success. Before you judge me, think about it, if you break your arm, you go see an orthopedic doctor. If you damage your vocal chords, you would go see a trained otolaryngologist [ear, nose and throat (ENT)] physician. When our emotions are injured, does it not make sense to go see a psychologist who is trained to help us heal psychologically? Some cultures place a negative stigma on seeing a psychologist, but let me assure you, when you connect with the right trained therapist, it is very healthy and freeing.

How many have heard the phrase, "*go where you're celebrated, not tolerated?*" That has been a point of reference for me in this process of rejection eradication. Knowing that you are valuable, first and foremost because you are a child of God, and that there is no one on this planet like you nor will there ever be. Be confident in knowing that whoever embraces you, be it friend, family member, future spouse, etc., they are embracing someone special! In case you didn't know it, *you are special*! For me, in my hometown, I felt too black to fit in there. Then when I moved to the DC, Maryland and Virginia area (DMV), I felt too white to fit in. I had to come to the realization that I grew up where I did and look the way I look, because God planned it to be that way. The same goes for you. You are who you are. You look the way you look. Don't apologize for it, embrace it. Of course, there are things that we can improve upon like our attitudes, responses to others and the like, but I'm referencing those things you cannot change.

FAITH FOR FIERY TRIALS

I have learned and am yet learning to thank God for what He did not allow to happen. I encourage you to do the same. What we see as rejection is often God's way of divinely protecting us and helping us to navigate to where we should be and to whom we should be connected. Feelings of rejection come in many forms which is why it is so crucial that we keep the lines of communication open between us and God. He will speak, but it's up to us to listen and obey!

Whew, I just said something right there! Sometimes, negative rejection comes because we simply did not want to crucify our flesh and walk away from a person, place or thing. The Bible says in 1 Corinthians 10:13 that, God will always give us a way of escape to let us know that we are headed down a path that could bring us mental, spiritual and sometimes even physical harm, but we feel, in our infinite wisdom (sarcastism intended) that we know what's best for our lives and we bypass all the signals telling us to stop ... leave ... or let go. So, we do it anyway, get rejected and then go through the vicious cycle of having to heal all over again! The sad truth is that rejection comes every day of our lives. It is how we process it that determines its effect on us. Today, I gift us with the gift of goodbye! To those who need this gift and accept this gift, unwrap it and use it often. Let's practice ... "Goodbye!" See, you feel better already, don't you? The only thing or person you need in life to survive is God. Therefore, if you are trying to hold on to someone or something that you *know* is not good for you, tell them . . . tell it goodbye! Your life will be so much better, and you will be so much freer for it!

As I close (that was so preachy—laughing out loud), I want to admonish you to *take back your power*! My psychologist constantly reminds me that I have to teach people how to treat me. The same applies to you. The responsibility is not on them to treat you better, the responsibility is yours. Former First Lady Eleanor Roosevelt, said it this way, "No one can make you feel inferior without *your* consent" (emphasis mine). I found that I was expecting others to give me something that they either did not have the capacity to give or were not willing to give; thereby I was placing false expectations on others. I became bitter. I came into agreement with the lies and behaviors that deceived me into believing that I was not valuable. Take back *your* power and acknowledge *your* worth. Forgive anyone who has hurt you and forgive yourself. You will then begin to truly walk in the beautifulness of who you were created to be. Embrace all of you! Place it all in God's hands, recognizing that His acceptance of you is what's most important.

I touch and agree with you now, in the Name of Jesus, that the root of rejection is eradicated in your life. I decree and declare freedom over you to be the beautiful person you were created to be! It may be a daily mental and spiritual fight, but *you are worth it*!

CRYSTAL Y. DAVIS

Tap into What's Already Inside of You

Growing up especially in the formative years, were you told that you could be whatever you wanted to be in life? As a seventies baby, I was told this over and over. If you think about what was going on culturally for African Americans, it was the period in which there was tremendous upswing as a result of the civil rights movement. As a people, we were finally reaping the benefits of the hope of our ancestors. My parents experienced more than their parents. Their desire for me and my sisters was that we would experience more than they did. It seems that no matter the oppression, each generation believed the next generation would accomplish more than the previous generation.

NICOLE S. MASON, ESQUIRE

Here's the Thing: Nobody Told Me the Road Would Be Easy!

As I reflect on my life prior to college, I grew up a bit naïve about life. However, college afforded me insights into just how much I didn't know or understand about how others grew up and what they had exposure to. I quickly learned that my purview was through rose colored glasses as it related to what I could accomplish in life. Here is my journey to greatness.

Throughout middle and high school, I was on the honor roll, very active in extra-curricular activities, took advanced courses, and worked a part-time job. Whether in academic studies, sports or band, my goal was to be at the top of my game. I wanted to be state champion in tennis, first chair in band and within the top 10 percent of my class—all of which I pursued or achieved. From a very young age, I strived to be a high achieving woman. It wasn't until life became difficult that I lost sight of these traits that were the foundation of my character. Traits that were already inside.

FAITH FOR FIERY TRIALS

The First Time the World Tried to Tell Me *No*

After I enrolled in college to pursue an engineering degree, I decided that I would skip the extracurricular activities that I had previously been involved in. I didn't try out for band or tennis. I wanted to focus on my education and adapting to this completely new and diverse environment.

Attending classes with 250 or more students, not having that sense of community I experienced growing up and grasping all this information, was very daunting. Additionally, I had many distractions socially. Let's just say that while I had a lot of fun, the foundation I had come to rely on had been shattered. The result was academic probation; the first time that I'd truly disappointed my parents and myself. Honestly speaking, it was the first time in my entire life that I was not sure that I could achieve what I set out to do. Not only was I struggling to keep up, I didn't like the course work, which made me question my choice of major. For nearly all of my teenage years, I declared that I wanted to be an engineer. Could I really spend 30 years of my life doing something I didn't enjoy? I decided that I would be an engineer—I just needed to determine the discipline that best fit who I wanted to become.

NICOLE S. MASON, ESQUIRE

The First Time I Truly Felt Like the *Only* One

As my classes became more focused on my major and smaller in size, I realized that often I was one of few women and the only African American. Again, I had to learn to forge new relationships as I searched for a study group. Remember, I was coming off academic probation. As a result, my confidence had been shaken. I didn't feel like the smart kid that could strongly and actively participate as I had done in the past. Added pressure was I didn't see many people who looked like me.

God gives us everything that we need. As I entered my third year of the five year program, a couple of students enrolled in the program from a historically black college. We, along with a few other African American students, formed an alliance and began to align on the courses we took and began a study group. This study group was my saving grace. My confidence rose, and that smart kid growing up was back.

FAITH FOR FIERY TRIALS

The First Time the World Tried to Tell Me That I Was *Not* Equal

The conference room was painted Caribbean blue. It was 1996 in Juarez, Mexico. I noticed the manufacturing manager was directing questions to my engineering colleague. I wasn't totally focused, because I assumed he was asking questions about his product line. However, my colleague began to ask me questions, and then respond to the manager. It occurred to me that this manager was directing questions for me through my colleague. *Wait*! He isn't addressing me!? Why? Is it because I'm African American? Female? Both? In 1996? *Seriously*!

All of this was happening in rapid succession in my mind. My range of emotions moved from shock and disbelief, to anger and then rage. I had to decide very quickly how I was going to respond. It didn't help that the work was stressful. We were working on a car platform that was behind schedule, yet the launch date did not change. The cultural differences and language barriers in a foreign country made matters worse. Did I mention that I didn't speak Spanish, and my lab technician didn't speak English? We didn't have a translator. My days were long and arduous. There were so many life changing elements occurring at the same time with very little time to focus on what I needed to adapt.

It was in that conference room that I knew that I had to act in a bold manner against this person's attempt to disqualify me. Although I knew his biases were rooted in either racism or sexism, I knew that the real issue was authority. I was only 26 years old at the time and learning and adapting to everything around me. I was angry. I wanted to jump across that table and strangle him. I wanted to read him from the top of his head to the sole of his feet, pop my neck and snap two fingers.

Thank God for Wisdom and Discernment

But God . . . I didn't forget my roots. I had reached a point in my life where I wanted a deeper relationship with God. This was my "Garden of Gethsemane" moment. Again, I was away from everything that felt familiar. I had friends, but I didn't have my family structure; lifelong connections. All that I had was God.

I fell in love with a small church where the teaching was rich. I can remember buying every type of Bible and supplement for study. I was determined to get back to center. At a time when so many things in my life were changing, there were times that I questioned myself. I was in a space where I wasn't certain who I was or who I was becoming.

I made a lot of mistakes in search of this new and maturing person. But through it all, God never left me. He always gave me what I needed when I needed it, despite my anxiety and attempts to preempt His timing.

I will admit that I didn't have the professional tact I have now as a mature woman, but I think I handled the situation well as a young professional. Recognizing that my authority was being tested, I quickly realized that I had the answers he needed. I expressed in a very firm and authoritative voice, that if he would not address me, his questions would go unanswered. I held the real power! He could not complete what he needed to do in manufacturing until my work went through a thorough process and series of tests, validations and approvals.

Making the wrong choice that day could have significantly altered the trajectory of my career. Had I dumbed myself down and spoken through a man in response to another man, I would have lost the respect of everyone in that room, including the entire male manufacturing staff. I thank God for the wisdom and courage to own my seat at the table.

NICOLE S. MASON, ESQUIRE

God You Got Jokes! Fast Forward Eighteen (18) Years

Sitting in a hotel room, in May of 2014, I wrote my resignation letter to corporate America. The time had come for me to make the leap into entrepreneurship. That day my boss called me in complete shock regarding my decision. My resignation wasn't based on any of the typical reasons. I wasn't angry, upset, or being mistreated. It was quite the opposite. The time had come for me to take up my cross.

The journey to this point started in 2003 when I knew without a doubt who I wanted to be. I didn't know how or when, but I was beyond certain that I wanted a boutique consulting firm. I had the great fortune to be mentored by a well-respected and successful influencer in the field. I told him about my dream to follow in his footsteps. He shared something that rocked my world. He told me that while he thought I could be successful because I was good at the practice, he didn't think I would be successful at business because decision makers expected to see someone like him—an older, established, experienced, retired, white man.

For some time, I believed what he said to be true. However, what I came to realize was that while it was reality at that time, it didn't have to be the reality of the future. At first, I blamed him for squashing my hopes. I knew in my heart of hearts that his honesty wasn't meant to hurt me. Upon reflection, I thank God for the information. Yet again, God revealed that information is power. Because my mentor shared that perspective, I could now work to combat it. It was indeed the fuel that I needed to change the narrative. And that is exactly what I worked to do. I started to equip myself with what I would need to be taken seriously; to be viewed as an expert and thought leader. I immersed myself in learning and perfecting my craft.

I decided that if I continued to take steps forward the day would come when the vision would be fulfilled. I started the company in 2009. I can recall being afraid, thinking that I needed to quit my job at that very moment. Yet there were so many things I didn't understand about business, like how to get clients, contracts, pricing, keeping clients, getting more clients, growing the business and so much more. After listing all these things, I almost talked myself out of starting the firm. I decided that if I did nothing else that I would legally start the company. That was my first real commitment to my dream.

I didn't see my first paying client until 2010. I was excited to receive the first check in the company name. I was ready . . . it was happening. At least I thought so! You can always depend on an obstacle when you think your situation is turning around.

Just when I was certain I was on the path to take the leap fully into the business, I was told that I was being considered for a promotion. I was amazed at how distracted I became by this news. I had worked extremely hard to lead the business unit to which I was assigned to achieve some very significant savings and efficiency targets. Several business units were duplicating and implementing our business prototype which ultimately became a company-wide model. In 2011, this body of work was acknowledged and shared as a best practice at the leading industry conference. This opportunity to promote the business prototype at the industry conference felt like my reward. However, the opportunity to share that accomplishment didn't manifest. As a matter of fact, although I was eligible and had been nominated for a promotion to the Vice President level, I was moved to another business unit to replicate the work. I was deeply disappointed, saddened and empty. I felt truly undervalued! Doubt crept in and the business dreams were back on the shelf. During that time, I became very bitter. I didn't like who I was becoming or how I felt. Again, my faith in God brought me out.

FAITH FOR FIERY TRIALS

Control What You Can Control

I was devastated when I didn't get the promotion after I had worked so hard to prove my worth and value. It was this statement, feeling and language that had me stuck. I realized that I didn't have to prove anything. All the work, the lessons learned, the people I influenced and developed, and the results achieved were still a part of me. That realization was the power that I needed to understand that I in fact was in control. I could choose how I responded to the situation. As a result, I let go of blaming the company for doing me wrong. I was still disappointed, which just meant that I needed to process through those emotions. It was the freedom that I needed to plan *my next*!

Two and a half short years after not being promoted, my dream was realized. I learned that the path in life isn't a straight line, but one filled with twists, turns, roadblocks, peaks and valleys. All of which prepare us for the unseen. I learned that life and people will try to make you fit in these perfectly designed boxes. These boxes, however, are designed by man, not God.

In Every Elevation and Life Promotion, Here Is What I Can Affirm

- *God never left me*—I had to learn to walk in the power and authority that He provided me.
- *God gave me everything I needed at the time I needed it.* When He commissions our path, he prepares the way. I had to learn to trust Him. There were times, when I was stressing about how to do something or to find a resource with a specific expertise. Then I would go to an event or to a friend's home, only to meet someone that could help me.
- *God revealed to me that information is power*! When I was younger my father always encouraged me to read. Of course, I didn't understand the power of this practice then. However, what I can affirm is that knowledge really is power, and it doesn't only come from books. It also comes from our experiences.

RENEE DANTZLER

Strength from Within

Growing up in a single parent home, I did not see an example of a wife. My mother did it all; she worked, paid bills, took care of my older sister and me, which included discipline. She was mom and dad. The one thing my mom did not do was take us to church. The occasions I went to church was either with my best friend and her mother or with my aunt. The absence of church was pivotal in shaping my view of marriage at a young age. I was extremely independent and liked making my own decisions. I did not know how to submit, neither was submission in my vocabulary. Submission sounded old fashioned and downright crazy if you asked me.

My husband and I met and dated in high school. One month after graduating from high school, we were married. We were young and had no idea what we were about to embark upon. We married because we knew that we loved each other and were expecting a baby. Exactly two months after we married I gave birth to our firstborn son, Andre. My husband joined the Navy and was in his Naval training school at the time of our son's birth. When Andre turned eight months old, we moved from New York to Virginia to join my husband who was already there serving in the U.S. Navy aboard a ship.

After completing four years in the Navy, my husband decided not to re-enlist. He did not like the fact that Andre rarely got to see him. We relocated to Texas and this was the true beginning of our marriage. Now the real test began. This is when we found out exactly what we were made of; no more going out to sea for three, four or even six months at a time. We would see each other *every single day*.

About six months after moving to Texas, my husband recommended that we start going to church. His suggestion came as no surprise to me since he grew up going to church. We started attending a small family Bible church and loved it. In April 1991, I made the best decision of my life; I gave my life to the Lord. I attended church services and Bible study regularly, and I became *stronger* in my faith. I started to understand the power of prayer and the power of words.

FAITH FOR FIERY TRIALS

It was still early in our marriage and right after giving my life to the Lord, all hell broke loose in my marriage. My husband and I were not getting along; we argued all the time. He often came home late from work. His pager was always going off and he would say, "It is work." I always felt as though something was not right, but I was naïve. Since I did not have proof of any wrong doing, I assumed that he was in fact working late. On a few occasions, I showed up at his job unannounced and would see him talking to a woman. I wasn't sure if it were my insecurities or if it was really something to it. I never saw any proof of infidelity, other than the fact that he seemed to be hanging out with this woman on his job. It wasn't until years later that my suspicion was indeed confirmed in marital counseling.

It is essential during trying times in our lives that we go to the *right* person for counsel. My "so called" friends told me to leave him. They said, "If I were you I would not put up with that." "If I were you, I would . . . " Most people do not have a clue what they would or would not do in various situations. Direction from God will always put you on the right path. "Blessed *is* the man who walks not in the counsel of the ungodly . . . " (Psalm 1:1 NKJV)

I decided to talk to my pastor's wife, Carol Young (God rest her soul). She taught me the power of words and encouraged me to fight for my marriage. She encouraged me to see him saved. Now that is having faith when what I saw at home was quite the contrary. She taught me to speak well of him. To decree, declare and claim victory despite what I saw or what appeared to be so. "My heart is overflowing with a good theme; I recite my composition concerning the King; My tongue *is* the pen of a ready writer." (Psalm 45:1 NKJV) She prayed with me and for me. She always encouraged me to continue to pray for my husband even when I didn't feel like it.

I spent many nights crying, then going to work stressed. I constantly felt like this was an indictment on me. It left me feeling as though I was not good enough, not pretty enough, not woman enough. Despite many threats and attempts to leave, the Lord always spoke to my heart to be still, and to stay *strong*. Leaving is easy; staying is hard and takes a *strong* woman to stick it out in the face of adversity. It was up to me to fight or flight. I had to have faith one day my husband would accept Jesus Christ as his personal Lord and Savior. The fight was not with my husband, the fight was and continues to be with the enemy. "For we do not wrestle against flesh and blood, but against principalities, against powers against the rulers of darkness of this age, against spiritual *hosts* of wickedness in the heavenly *places*." (Ephesians 6:12 NKJV)

As time went by God continued working on me. I did not see any changes in my husband, but I was determined to follow God's Word. This strengthened my faith and I started to look at things and myself differently. A different perspective helped me to see things with faith and not fear. I began to make faith confessions over my husband and my marriage. "He loves the Lord and serves God in ministry." "He loves me the way Christ Loves the church." "He is ready for church ahead of me" (Now that this is a reality it can be a point of contention, so be careful what you pray for). I confessed, "My husband loves me more today than he ever did." "Husbands, love your wives, just as Christ also loved the church and gave Himself for her . . . " (Ephesians 5:25 NKJV) My confession was, "My husband adores me, appreciates and respects me." It is important to note, do not just make the positive confessions, but believe what you confess. I learned to call those things that be not as though they were; decreeing and declaring my husband was a man of integrity, a man of God, honoring me and faithful to the ministry of a Husband. "Death and life are in the power of the tongue, And those who love it will eat its fruit." (Proverbs 18:21 NKJV) God was teaching me how to pray and to be steadfast, unmovable and always abounding in the work of the Lord.

Learning how to forgive my husband and rebuild trust after infidelity in my marriage was definitely a test of my faith in God. This process did not happen overnight. The reality for forgiveness is it is not for the offender, it is for the offended. Forgiveness is the art of making an intentional decision to change ill feelings about an offense. How could I expect God to forgive me if I did not forgive my husband? Aphiemi, the Greek translated word in the Bible for forgiveness means, "let it go." This faithful act is pleasing to God.

There were many occasions while my husband and I were at church listening to the Word, I thought to myself, "I hope he is getting this," or "This is a good Word for him." I was sitting there hoping something was said or done to change him or make him a better husband. One Sunday, the Holy Spirit convicted me. The Holy Spirit said to me, "You need to listen to the Word for you!" "Stop waiting for the perfect Word for your husband or someone else." "You need to hear from Me for yourself, you need to change." "Therefore, my beloved, as you have always obeyed, not as in my presence only, but now much more in my absence, work out your own salvation with fear and trembling . . . " (Philippians 2:12 NKJV). The times I sat there saying, "This Word is good for him," or "I hope he is getting it," I was missing what the Lord was saying to help me be a better wife and better person. The fact remained I could not change my husband, God had to do it. I could only change myself. The Holy Spirit gave me a shocking revelation, *I am not perfect*. While I was trying to change my husband, I had areas of improvements to make on myself. Such improvements would motivate my mate to change or react differently in some circumstances.

At the advice of my Pastor's wife, I started spending more time in prayer and reading my Bible. When he came home from work instead of complaining about what took him so long or a bill was due, I would greet him with a hug and kiss. More frequently, he would come home to find me reading the Word or preparing dinner. At first my efforts seemed to go unnoticed. The Holy Spirit was working on me.

Despite our ups and downs that did not stop us from getting pregnant. God blessed me to give birth to our second son, Anthony, in 1992. In fact, having my son at this time in our marriage was definitely divine timing, because God made it challenging for me to leave. Do not get it twisted, I still had moments when I thought about it, but God never allowed it. Now that I was pregnant this was a test to my character. Managing my emotions took great inner strength. About a year after giving birth to Anthony, my husband gave his life to the Lord. Gradually, I began to see changes in him. All the faith confessions began to manifest before my very eyes. We started serving together at church. We sang in the choir together, headed our Witnessing Team, Clothing and Food Bank Ministry. God exceeded my expectations. Now that Doug dedicated his life to the Lord everything will be perfect; no more troubles, right? Yeah, right!

After suffering a miscarriage a few years later, it was a difficult time for us. That year was very challenging. I frequently asked myself if it was my fault. I had to find strength yet again to trust God and His will. My husband remained strong and was a great encouragement to me. A year later, the Lord blessed us yet again to get pregnant and give birth to our third son Andrew in 1998.

In July of 2012, I received a diagnosis of Ductal Carcinoma in Situ, also known as DCIS, an early stage of breast cancer located in the ducts of the breast. I was only forty-two years old at the time of the diagnosis and there is no history of cancer in my family. This was a frightening time. My husband held my hand every step of the way. From the diagnosis, through two lumpectomy procedures and radiation, my husband was there. When fear crept up on me, he prayed, he encouraged me, and he kept me going. All the seeds of prayer I planted over my husband and the tears that watered them continues to reap a harvest for me in my marriage. I thank God for my husband.

"Have you considered my servant's Douglas and Renee?" Just like Job in the Bible, I truly believe God had this conversation with the devil regarding my husband and me. On July 8, 2016, our youngest son, our baby, Andrew went home to be with the Lord. He passed two months after his eighteenth birthday and one month after graduating from high school. I have had my share of trials from financial struggles, infidelity, breast cancer and now losing our youngest child. How much more can a person take God? God is trusting us with pain knowing despite the gravity of it, we will stay *strong* enough to trust and serve Him. Our journey of grief begins. How can I find strength in this? The pain is indescribable, the void, the emptiness, the hurt, the anger, the disappointment . . . the grief. How does one survive such a tremendous loss? How can I continue living my life with a part of me gone? The Lord spoke to my spirit, "One moment, one breath, one step and one day at a time." After all, I do have a husband and two other sons who need me as much as I need them. Once again, I need to discover new strength from within. "Have I not commanded you? Be *strong* and of good courage; do not be afraid, nor be dismayed, for the Lord your God *is* with you wherever you go." (Joshua 1:9 NKJV) When Andrew passed away, a big part of me went with him. Despite the pain, I must continue to live my life in such a way that someday I will hear the Lord say, "Well done thy good and faithful servant," and I will see my son again. Until the day the Lord calls me home, Rest in Paradise (RIP) Andrew David Dantzler. Mommy loves you, Mommy misses you and will continue to be *strong* in the Lord! "You've already decided how long we'll live—You set the boundary and no one can cross it." (Job 14:5 MSG)

As a certified personal trainer, I am accustomed to helping my clients lift weights in order to complete an exercise safely and successfully. This concept in weight training is known as "spotting." Spotting is the act of supporting another person during weight lifting, with an emphasis on allowing the participant to lift or push more than they could normally do effectively and safely, without the additional support. My husband is my spotter in life. He helps me to carry loads and weights that I otherwise could not lift or carry alone.

In January of 2018, after taking some time to grieve our son's death, my husband and I returned to teaching pre-marital counseling class at our church. It is our mission to help as many couples as possible to find strategies to stay together and stay strong. We believe that marriage works if you work it. Although our journey of grief continues, we stay strong by continuing the work of the Lord together. My husband and I are a team and we are stronger together. God is the source of our strength!

DR. VIKKI JOHNSON

There Should Have Been Four

When I was a little girl I wanted to get married to the man of my dreams and have seven children. I always wanted to have a big family. However, it didn't happen that way. My journey to who I am today has been a privately complex one, even though it may have looked easy to others. I served others publicly but struggled alone, privately. I helped others create peace in their lives while suffering in my own personal chaos. As an athlete I learned how to "show up" for the game and play even if I was in pain. During that time in my life when I was focused on pretending to be okay; I mastered the "game face." Today I dance to my own music and I no longer pretend to be well if I am not.

NICOLE S. MASON, ESQUIRE

My daughter is the absolute joy of my life. She is a precious gift from God, and I thank Him every day for entrusting me with her. At the same time, I can't help but think how different my life would be if the other three—yes, three children—I conceived had been born and a part of my world today. It makes me pause, even as I write this, to imagine "what could have been" if I was now the mother of three daughters (32, 24, 19) and one son (21) at this time in my life. It is amazing how easily I recall their birth order and their ages.

My first pregnancy ended in a miscarriage. I remember that period in my life like it was yesterday. I was a junior in college, on a full athletic scholarship, a member of the gospel choir, and my sorority was in the midst of pledging a line. I was excited about being pregnant. I was so excited that I was fearless. I was ready to defend my decision to have a baby despite what it would cost me. I was willing to walk away from my basketball scholarship, from people's opinions, and even from the people who were the most disappointed in me.

My relationship with the baby's father had become contentious, and he wanted me to have an abortion. I adamantly refused telling him that he could leave at that very moment and never come back. The baby and I would be fine even if I had to do it alone. I remember the night shortly thereafter that I went into premature labor at 12 weeks. It was 1986. I had been hanging out with some of my girlfriends and started cramping really badly. I thought if I rested it would pass. About three hours later the pain got worse, and my friend took me to the hospital because when I went to the bathroom, I was bleeding badly.

I was in the emergency room alone very nervous and uncertain of what was going on. I was alone in the examining room and remember making a conscious, sincere commitment to the Lord. That night my relationship with God truly began and He let me know that He was with me, even when the baby's father wasn't. My parents were hours away and no one knew where I was except my friend who brought me to the emergency room.

That night I went through hours of painful labor with no anesthesia. I remember literally wailing for what seemed like an eternity and begging for help from the nurses who seemed to ignore my suffering. I just wanted the pain to stop—even if it meant death. I just wanted the pain to stop! Eventually a nurse came to see about me. She gently rubbed my forehead trying to console me; however, I was inconsolable. It was something about the way she was looking into my eyes that let me know what was happening to me was not good. I began to whimper and swallow my sobs because in the absence of medical confirmation of what was happening to me I somehow knew that at 21 years old I was alone and losing the baby girl I had started planning my life around.

Many hours later I had a surgical procedure to complete the miscarriage. Was God punishing me even though I had made a commitment to Him that night? *It was horrible*! The mental and emotional trauma lasted for years, but I kept showing up in my life like everything was fine. I suppressed my grief and went back to playing basketball. I felt so horrible about myself and my life that I remained in the relationship that had produced this child another year even though it was unhealthy.

Two years later I got married to someone I barely knew. I had become heavily involved in a small church that encouraged young people to get married. I didn't know then, but I know now I was still numb from the previous trauma, so I went with it. I was married one year after breaking up with my baby's father. Seven years after my miscarriage and five years after my wedding, I had a beautiful daughter in 1993.

I barely remember the first five years of her life because I suffered with postpartum depression. That's what suppressed anger will do for you. It was awful. As I reflect on those moments right after childbirth, I remember not wanting to hold her or breastfeed her or have her in the hospital room with me. I was angry for having to endure seven hours of feeling like someone was hitting me in my lower back with a hammer. Thank God my mother, cousin and a few good friends were around me those first weeks. I needed them more than I realized. They were all my angels on assignment. As crazy as it sounds, I was also angry at my newborn because I concluded that she reminded me of my inadequacies and inability to have the baby I miscarried five years earlier.

I was in a deep, dark hole and didn't know how I was going to get out. It took me about four years to work through this "wilderness experience" without any drugs, therapy or social media. God delivered me in a moment. I didn't understand what I was going through until after God healed me. I was a mess and still nurturing unhealed wounds.

Two years after the birth of my daughter, I got pregnant from someone I loved, and it was not my husband. The relationship was a secret. I was so lost in my chaos of pain I was imploding. Things were getting worse, not better. It's ironic how "before accepting Christ" I was fearless, courageous, and willing to go through the fire to have my baby. This time it was different. I was scared, alone and fearful. I was bound by thoughts of shame, humiliation, rejection, intimidation, abandonment and other people's opinions. What would the church people think? I was over the youth ministry. What would I tell my pastor and his wife? What would my family think about the "golden child?" The baby's father was caught in the same web of questions. He persuaded me that we had "too much to lose" if I had the baby. After deep contemplation I had an abortion. I aborted our son, another baby I wanted badly. The baby's father paid for the abortion and that was the extent of his involvement. As far as I'm concerned, I went through it alone. Once again, God let me know that He was with me, even if the baby's father wasn't.

At first, I felt relief. Then the thoughts of regret, anger, resentment, hurt, and loss began to periodically overwhelm me. What had I done? Why did I do it? I had an abortion so *everybody else* would be okay. What about me? There I was "in Christ" where I should have been the most secure, yet this left me feeling insecure and fragile. I wondered if this was something I would have to deal with for the rest of my life.

Believe it or not a couple more years passed, and I was doing okay until I got pregnant *again* in yet another "secret relationship." This time I thought about what I wanted and how happy this baby would make me. That did not last long. The baby's father and

FAITH FOR FIERY TRIALS

I were both married to other people. Too many people would be hurt. Too many lives would be affected and thrust into turmoil. I thought about taking my daughter, running away, and having the baby on my own. You know, desperate people do desperate things, right? Who was I kidding? I could not do that either. So, after much thought and discussion with the baby's father, I convinced myself *again* that aborting our unborn daughter was the best thing for everybody else. The relief only lasted a few hours this time. Later that same day, the waves of guilt and regret began to wash over me with an intensity that lasted for the next several months.

I remember attending my Grandmother's funeral during this time and completely breaking down as soon as I saw her in the casket. Yes, I was sad that she was gone, but for the first time, I felt the anguish of conceiving and not having three babies. After that one good breakdown at the wake, I would only cry if no one else was around. I hid my pain from people. Once again, God let me know that He was there.

Years later I cried out to God telling Him how sorry I was for rejecting His gifts. I also told God that I needed His help because I could no longer live like this. The guilt was secretly taking over my life. The first thing God did was "turn up" His love for me through my daughter. She was and still is my angel.

The next thing God did was allow me to hear a Christian radio broadcast. I was driving to work one morning listening to Pastor Jack Hayford as he ministered to women who had experienced abortions. I was stunned. His words were very soothing. He encouraged listeners to request his book entitled, *I'll Hold You In Heaven*. That book was the beginning of my healing. The reassurance that I will see my children again is what provoked me to go after God with all that's within me.

These days I'm learning that in order to receive more from God, we must create capacity by releasing what no longer serves us. When I gave up doing things my way, God showed me a better way. I held on to some things too long even though they were not good for me. I did not know my life would take the path it has taken. If left up to me I would have had the storybook life of a beautiful home, the perfect husband and seven well-mannered children. I have walked a path that has included lots and lots of pain and many years of uncertainty. I have not always made the best decisions, but I have tried to honor the lessons I have learned as an example of survival to women everywhere.

Each time I conceived, my children became a part of me forever. I still have "moments" every now and then. The difference now is that I fully embrace and engage the love of God. The security and reassurance found in that love made provisions for my mistakes and bad choices. His love forgives me and enables me to forgive myself. I can't stop the moments of regret from coming, but I don't invite them to stay around either. The last thing I did (and maybe this will help someone), was create a memorial for the children I conceived that didn't make it here. It's not important what the memorial is as much as it is imperative that you create one. You can plant a garden, add charms to your bracelet/necklace, and start a project or business in your child's or children's memory. Whatever you do, don't act like it never happened because it did. Honor your child's memory in a way that is meaningful to you. There are many options. The beauty is, that this time you choose something that brings life.

MINISTER SHARRON JAMISON

Healing My Son and Me

It was over seventeen years ago, but I can still remember the pain of seeing my son frightened, bruised and battered. There he stood, his face swollen, tear-stained eyes with a look of bewilderment on his face. I couldn't move; I was stunned. Seeing him like that was painful, almost unbearable. His six-year-old vocabulary was too limited to fully express what happened and how he felt, but I knew. Even though I wished I did not know, I knew. The images of his small frame being hit, pushed and kicked by fourth-, fifth-, and sixth-grade boys in a school bathroom made me wince, because I knew. I felt as if I had been punched in the stomach; I felt angry as hell. I didn't feel sad. I felt sorrowful. I knew that his experience if not addressed, would be a defining moment in his life. I didn't want to know, but I knew.

My initial response had to appear rather odd to the school officials. I stared at them, but I was looking through them and straining to look into my son's soul. I was struggling to wake up because some parts of me thought I was dreaming. Or, maybe I was just having a flashback, some kind of out of body experience. Was I hallucinating? Did this actually happen?

I could not wrap my head around what transpired; I could not digest it all. I just stood there in a daze. I realized my body and brain were telling me to say something, but I couldn't. I could not think. Words escaped me. The pain was too deep, too raw, and too real; I was paralyzed.

Seeing my son's injured face was agonizing. I wanted to touch it, but I couldn't. I didn't know what to do, and so I just grabbed my son and hugged him tight. I wanted him to know that he was safe, mommy was there. I wanted to take the pain away. I wanted to erase the experience from his memory. I wanted to give him my strength. I wanted him to feel loved. I wanted revenge. I wanted my mommy. But most of all, I didn't want my son, my only child, to hurt now or suffer later. I wanted none of that.

I could not believe that my son had been assaulted. I knew he had to have been terrified. I struggled not to visualize the blows to his body or the hits to his face. Even though I didn't want to imagine the pain, I knew. I knew because the same situation happened to me almost 35 years ago. I knew and knowing tortured me.

The school officials attempted to explain what happened. I don't remember what they said because it didn't matter. They tried to give me some sort of explanation, but any rationale was insufficient. Let's be honest, what could a six-year-old boy have done to deserve being attacked in the bathroom while he changed his clothes? What could a six-year-old boy have done to warrant being jumped by a gang? What could a six-year-old boy have done to encourage older boys to harass and hurt him? What could a six-year-old boy have done that warranted his teacher neglecting to immediately notify me that he had not only been hurt, but traumatized? What?

There were no good answers; none of the school's politically-correct I don't want-to-get sued statements contained any empathy or concern. No justification or rationale assuaged my pain or answered any of my questions. My son was a six-year-old first grader. Nothing could have provoked such an attack. Nothing could have warranted him being hit with so much force that this face was badly swollen; my son looked like he had a mouth full of rocks. No one could have appreciated that this two to three minute attack could take twenty to thirty years to heal; overcoming trauma takes time.

My son wasn't a bully. He was not part of a gang. He was not devoid of love, home training, or parental support. I made sure that he had the best, the best of everything, especially the best of me. What could have motivated a group of boys to use my son's body as a punching bag and his face for boxing practice? Could they have just been bullies looking for a victim and my son was simply their unfortunate patsy of the day? What?

The sad truth was that my son was assaulted because he was black. Yes, he was a black male child with an Arabic name in a white, Christian school that supposedly promised and promoted love. That was his offense; his color. His color made him a target for home-bred hate. His color made him defenseless against cruelty. His color made him vulnerable to abuse. His color exposed his teachers to be neglectful, uncaring, and unaware that his blackness threatened his own safety. That's the truth. But of course, that's not the truth the school acknowledged.

I had my reservations about moving to Kentucky and enrolling my son in a Christian school. But I dispelled my misgivings despite the state's reputation for being biased. I was optimistic and open-minded. I trusted the school's vision, the principal's dedication, and teacher's supervision. Since it was a Christian school, I expected that Godly principles would be taught and demonstrated. I thought that school officials would be fair and exemplify the "love your neighbor as yourself" commandment. I assumed. I hoped. I prayed.

Despite my own painful childhood experiences, my own suspicion, and my intuition, I trusted the Baptist Christian School to care for my son. I trusted, but really prayed, that his educational experience would be different. I wanted, but really needed, his educational experience to be positive, fun and joyful and not full of fear, humiliation and isolation like mine. I didn't want him to grow up with no self-worth, no self-esteem, minimal self-knowledge or no self-love. I knew the dangers of not cultivating a healthy self-concept, and I knew the consequences of not having sufficient affirmation. I knew what it meant to be without acceptance, validation or celebration. I knew because it was my experience. I didn't want to know, but I knew.

Eventually, the hiding, driving, and working took its toll. I was physically tired and emotionally drained. My great-paying consultant position lost its allure, and I wanted out. I wanted my son to feel safe. I wanted to sleep, and the constant anxiety started to affect my mental health. I decided to move. I was out of Kentucky. I hated it, and I was growing bitter by the day.

I explained what happened to my son to my directors. However, senior management refused to transfer me; they had just relocated me to Kentucky less than one year before. They issued me an ultimatum; stay in Kentucky or resign. I was fine with those options. I was not deterred; I was moving. My son's safety and my health were not negotiable; my sanity was at stake. When I announced I was leaving, they agreed to transfer me if I financed the relocation.

What senior management didn't realize was that I didn't need nor was I waiting for their permission. I had already updated my resumé, contacted my clients, put my home on the market, and I researched new schools for my son. No one was going to determine my son's future; I was the parent, and I was the provider, not a company.

My move back to Florida was difficult, to say the least. For more than 11 months, I had two mortgages which drained my savings. I had a traumatized son who was extremely distraught and having nightmares. He was acting out; he was hurting. I didn't blame him at all. He was grieving, humilated and angry but did not understand how to process it all. Who would know?

FAITH FOR FIERY TRIALS

How do you explain to a six-year-old that his color caused his beating? How do you explain to a six-year-old boy that his last name gave a few fools a license to assault him? How do you explain to a little boy that adults colluded and protected the abusers, with little concern for his well-being? You explain as much as you can so that your child does not hate himself or others. Then, you work as fast as you can to create normalcy, rehabilitate his soul, and provide support; you start the healing journey.

The healing journey was painful (yes healing hurts), and I learned three powerful lessons about life.

1. ***Always do what is best for you.*** Often people are quick to give advice without knowing or appreciating the variables of a situation. Listen to your soul and don't forget that it is *you* who must deal with the consequences of your decisions, not the advisors. Listen to wise counsel but always make the final decisions in your life. Don't abdicate authority to others. It is your life; you have to live it.

2. ***Always listen to your intuition, which I know is God's voice.*** I must admit that hearing your soul is not always easy, especially when your ego screams while your soul whispers. But

listen! Get quiet and get still. God will speak to you. God will use words, signs, people and dreams. Listen. God will direct your path.

I didn't listen to my intuition, and my son suffered. My intuition told me not to move; stay in Florida. My ego said to accept the consultant position in Kentucky; build your resumé. My intuition said the school does not feel right; blacks are not welcome. My ego said the school has a great aftercare program which would give me flexibility with my job. My intuition said your son is not being treated fairly. My ego said to make money and advance your career. My ego was loud, and the voice from my soul was muted. Pain resulted.

3. ***Forgive yourself quickly.*** My son suffered, and I suffered. I wallowed in guilt. I felt ashamed. I was full of regret. I felt stupid. I felt hopeless. I felt unfit to be his mother. I was numb; I wanted to escape, I wanted to hide. I was so guilt-ridden that I stopped parenting him. I stopped disciplining him. I stopped preparing him for manhood. I was failing, floundering and forsaking him. I didn't realize that his experience had torn off

the scabs of my own healing. His experience transported me back to my painful past, and I got trapped in my own childhood trauma. I was in agony, and I was sinking fast. He was hurting. I was hurting. We both needed help; we were both grieving. We were both suffering.

But, I had to forgive. I had to forgive myself and accept responsibility for my decisions. Not until I forgave myself for making bad decisions did I start the healing process. And not until I healed, did I become a parent again. And not until I became a parent again, could I support his healing.

Forgiveness initiated *our* healing journey. It was a difficult and slow process, and in some ways, my son is still healing. Gratefully, forgiveness was the elixir that paved the way to our restoration and recovery.

My son's attack was one of the hardest times in my life, but I made it. Even though I was drowning in despair, too ashamed to ask for help and too overwhelmed with my son's care, I persevered. I worked every day and persisted through the very pain that threatened my sanity. Quitting wasn't an option.

Some days I struggled. However, adversity did not stop me, uncertainty did not scare me, and the lack of finances didn't deter me. I knew that everything we needed on our healing journey was within me. I'm not sure how I knew, but I knew because I knew God.

Sometimes you don't realize that your childhood wounds have not healed. You think painful feelings and memories are resolved until something triggers you and transports you back to those painful places. Once transported, you are forced to look deeply into your soul. You are forced to courageously face the experiences and events that shaped you.

My son's attack forced me to analyze my soul, and I discovered untreated wounds. I identified emotional sores that were festering with anger, shame, bitterness and sadness. I saw a little girl hiding, powerless, hopeless and helpless. I saw images of me that I thought were buried. I sought professional help.

My son's attack was traumatic. It changed him, me and our relationship. We grew closer, wiser and stronger. We grew spiritually, and by God's grace, his attack did not cause irreparable harm to his spirit or soul.

I believe our pain equips us for our purpose. It is during the worst times in our lives that we are strengthened, prepared to serve humanity and to answer our divine call. When I healed from the pain of my childhood and from my son's attack, I became an advocate for healing because I believe healing frees people from depression and dysfunction. Emotional healing cultivates compassion, clarity, courage and connection. Emotional healing closes the past and holds unlimited promise for the future. Emotional healing illuminates and elevates! Emotional healing resurrects and restores. It revives, renews and rejuvenates.

The journey to wholesomeness was layered and long. I grieved, I yelled, I prayed, and I bargained. I read the Bible to find answers, solutions, solace and guidance. I opened my heart and allowed God to usher me through the healing process.

God, who is our Father, was there reminding me of His goodness, grace and mercy. The words and prayers that I learned in my father's church soothed and comforted me as I rebuilt our life.

The journey was not easy; flashbacks happened at the most inopportune times, but we made it. Thank God my son and I made it. *To God be the glory*! Blessings!

KISHA MARTIN-BURNEY

Fear, Faith and Restoration: A Married Woman's Testimony

I am writing from a place of peace, giving God the glory for helping me to stay in a solid and sound state of mind.

All I have ever known was how wonderful it was to be surrounded by my family all the time. I have always wanted to be in a fulfilling relationship like my mom and dad. I considered myself fortunate, able to experience being raised by both of my parents, unlike many of my peers. I imagined my life as a mother and wife would be very similar to my parents, because I was constantly surrounded by their love and affection for one another. My parents were 16 and 17 when I was born. They, too, were supported by their families, which made raising me easier. It was always my belief that I was destined to nurture the same type of relationship. Why not?

I was raised smart, intelligent and independent—values my parents instilled in me from a very young age. My father always taught me to depend on myself and always have a back-up plan for everything. My mother taught me to be caring, kind, loving and to "Treat people the way you want to be treated."

At 19, I moved out on my own, because I could not deal with my father's strictness. I was determined to prove I could make a decent life for myself. I moved in with my boyfriend, who turned out to be possessive, obsessive and who wanted full control of my life. What I thought was freedom and independence, turned into a complete nightmare.

There were many twists and turns as I was trying to find myself, fit in and to belong. I had a void. The strange part about it was that my father was always active in my life, so I could not understand where this void came from. Lord knows, I was looking for love in what appeared to be in all of the wrong places. I started to question whether or not I was worthy of being in a good relationship.

I met Mr. D. at a club one night through a mutual friend. At the time, I thought he was Godsent, perfect and made my heart skip a beat! After several months, we became very comfortable hanging out, partying and enjoying life. I lost connection with most of the world, my parents, family and church. I wouldn't say I was in church faithfully anyways, but it was one of the farthest things from my mind.

Seek and ye shall find. "There is no fear in love; but perfect love casts out fear . . . " (1 John 4:18 NKJV). After experiencing failed relationships and feeling rejected, I finally decided to find a place of my own. I was 20 years old and living in my own place. I was fearful of the unknown but determined to find myself. I also attempted to fit in with the "status quo," by going to college. I was employed by the U.S Department of State, as was my mother. Yes Lord, I was starting to accomplish some things in life. I was living, partying, and enjoying life with no children or unwanted responsibilities. I felt like I had "arrived."

On the flip side of things, Mr. D. was going through a separation with a girlfriend and I thought it was perfect timing. I jumped in to save the day and offered Mr. D. a place to live, which he graciously accepted. Did I not learn my lesson the first time after living with a boyfriend? This was different. That's what I told myself and I was going to do whatever it took to make this relationship work!

NICOLE S. MASON, ESQUIRE

And the Journey Began

After months of living together, I became pregnant. I was on an emotional rollercoaster, going from being happy, to sad and fearful. It became evident and clear to me that I needed to make our relationship official, and I was determined to not have any kids out of wedlock. After all, I wanted my kids to experience the same type of relationship as I had experienced with my parents! Unfortunately, Mr. D. did not share in my enthusiasm. It turned out that he was not ready for this type of commitment. Wedding bells were ringing in my ears. I couldn't imagine it any other way. Instead of a traditional, one-knee proposal, it became a planned arrangement. I never took a moment to consider God's plan for my life.

The scripture reads, "He who finds a wife finds a good thing, And obtains favor from the Lord." (Proverbs 18:22 NKJV). Knowing what I know now, this is the law that we should all live by when marriage is being considered. Of course, I wanted my parents to be proud that I was going to have a family and not be a single mother. I sincerely thought I was doing what my parents and God wanted me to do. However, getting pregnant out of wedlock was the first mistake; then attempting to make it right after the damage was done, was totally out of order.

FAITH FOR FIERY TRIALS

I was determined to be the best wife and mother that I could be. All along I thought I was doing what God wanted me to do. As far as I knew, Mr. D. never freely expressed his relationship with God, although he did speak often about Allah. In the midst of all the chaos of getting married and having a baby, not once did I step back and give my future husband the chance to choose me (See Proverbs 18:22). I also neglected to get to know my husband's family and his roots. Little did I know that these were important factors that could eventually sabotage my family's future!

As life went on, I realized that things had just "got real" and each day became more difficult. Doing things out of order certainly came with many obstacles and challenges. My son Q was born two months early and weighed only 2.3 lbs. I had initially planned on getting married before his arrival. I was conflicted with all kinds of thoughts. I asked myself: "Was my son's early birth due to me doing things out of order?" "Was this a result of my disobedience?" "Jesus, talk to me!" As I laid in the hospital on bed rest, I was scared, confused, and with plenty of time to meditate. Shortly thereafter, I became Mrs. Addison, a name I would surely pass on to my children proudly. I could not help but feel defeated.

I was scared, but I confessed that things would get better. I prayed to God to forgive me for my sins and give me the strength to make things right for the sake of my family. After all, God knew my heart! Moving on and finding comfort in knowing, "This too shall pass," was all a figment of my imagination.

The following year, it was time to move with my family into a bigger home. I was determined to have the best life for my family. Again, I was not convinced that Mr. D. felt the same way. This was all starting to feel orchestrated. Mr. D. was working as a part-time barber and attending school full-time.

I decided to maintain a full-time job with benefits and a decent salary to support my family. Never once did I think that my husband was supposed to be holding his family down. I stayed the course, convincing myself that things would get better. I wasn't being true to my feelings. I buried my own needs for those of my family. I was too vested to think about doing anything different, even though I was feeling unhappy in my marriage since day two.

As I sat reflecting and looking over my life, I realized I was living a big fat lie. In fact, while I was on bed rest Mr. D. did not stay overnight even though I was in the hospital for two weeks. Overall, Mr. D. was disconnected and had very little input when it came to making decisions for our family.

Slowly, signs of infidelity began to surface, which I refused to accept. This was a very scary place.

FAITH FOR FIERY TRIALS

Again, I maintained a positive attitude again saying, "This too shall pass." I did not have a good relationship with my mother-in-law and neither did Mr. D. Not only did I not have a relationship with my mother-in-law, but I didn't know any other members of Mr. D's family; not one person with the last name Addison. This should have been some type of indication of his roots, unlike with my family; he knew them all well. Mr. D. was welcomed into my family as if they were his very own.

Our life was merely about surviving and existing. Our routine was the same, day in and day out. I worked 40 to 60 hours per week while he attended school. Again, with the process of moving and helping Mr. D. find a job after graduating, which was challenging, I encouraged him to press on, rolled my sleeves up and helped him find a job in his field. I prayed for him every step of the way, never losing faith. I was deeply invested in our family's success. I even arranged his financing for school. I had all the answers and if I didn't, I would find them. I had unconsciously moved into the head of household role.

I found comfort in staying busy, looking past the downsides of my marriage and ignoring how truly unhappy I was. My emotions and life seemed like a rollercoaster. Fearful at one moment, faithful the next! It was definitely my faith that kept me going. I never felt secure in my marriage. It was as if I was operating in sort of blind faith.

As I stepped back to re-evaluate my future career goals which I had neglected, especially since I had been so busy giving so much of myself, I had a revelation that I had never given this area of my life too much thought. In 1996, I started a job at Sprint. There, I met my now husband, CB, who became a great friend and confidant. Apparently, Mr. D. had found comfort in building relationships outside of our marriage and was too busy to notice.

We no longer put much time into being husband and wife. After all, I was so busy making sure that my family was okay, that I lost myself. We began to grow further and further apart. The guilt of our infidelity started to grow obvious as time passed. Mr. D. and I agreed to go our separate ways, but let others and *fear* talk us out of it, since divorce should not be an option. I assumed I was making the right decision.

Again, I Was Back to Living a Lie

In 1998, our second child JC was born. She was the daughter I had been longing to have and she brought me so much joy. Seeing her little face made me think differently and again, I thought this was the reason that God kept us together. The philosophy of having children doesn't necessarily keep marriages together. If the family bond is not solid, it can make situations more difficult. I thought JC was our love child, but again, we ended up being right back to square one—in a circle of lies and deception which eventually ended with an inevitable divorce.

The separation and divorce was the ugliest thing that I had ever experienced. Mr. D. who was never committed to our marriage just stayed the course, as long as I kept laying things out for him. So, why not? I didn't love myself enough to feel worthy of having a husband who would ultimately put me first and take care of me. After all, he did not find me. I was not his rib. As I stated earlier, this was an arrangement. I offered marriage. I bought my own wedding ring. I purchased our home. I arranged for his tuition to get paid. I put everything in my name, which ultimately left me in a great deal of debt. Ours was not an amicable separation. In fact, the separation and the divorce was harsh. He refused to co-parent and blamed me for everything that went wrong. How was that? I sacrificed my entire life, but what I did not do was consult God first!

Restored

After many hardships, raising my kids on my own, and not having a good relationship with their father, I was determined to get my life back. I went from being in fear to having faith in finding a way to restore my life. I repented, prayed and built an everlasting relationship with God. I put God first, consulted him and trusted him with every forthcoming decision that I was destined to make in my life. Lord knows if I had only done this in the beginning, I would have saved myself a lot of heartache and pain.

Q went through a lot, because he was the oldest and was affected the most. Our son became angry, especially when he felt the rejection of his father. Unfortunately, Mr. D. wasn't there for our son, but I kept praying and I still am. Q decided to join the Army Reserves and is now living on his own.

JC is now a sophomore in college, despite her father's resistance to help with her college tuition. I truly didn't know how I was going to make it happen. Mr. D. scolded me for not saving child support to pay for JC's education. The devil is a liar! I often wonder how he proposed that I take care of the children and save the same money to pay for JC's college education!

Q and JC are the sources of my strength. Although faced with many obstacles, generational curses will be broken, and my kids shall live quality lives and continue to rise. I thank God every day for blessing me with them!

Yes, I had to sell my home, move five to eight times, transfer my kids' schools, change jobs and much more, but when I tell you that there was light at the end of the tunnel, I saw it! My faith had been restored, "Therefore, if anyone *is* in Christ, *he* is the new creation; old things have passed away; behold, all things have become new." (2 Corinthians 5:17 NKJV). It was time that I forgave myself and I came to understand that as I confessed to God my sins and asked for forgiveness, I could freely move on and live the life that I deserved!

I decided to become a full-time Real Estate Agent, having obtained my license in 2002. This was my passion. I decided to invest in myself for a change and do something that I truly loved.

In 2014, I married my long-time friend and confidant, CB, who has shown me from the first day we met that I am a queen and should be treated as such. He supports me, is a great father to his own children and step-father to mine. He consulted my father first to ask for my hand in marriage. I knew his parents extremely well and members of his extended family. I consulted God first. Our families were very much alike. Like my parents, his parents have been together since high school; so, we were cut from very similar cloths. Everything that presented itself in my path going forward was definitely a sign that God was certainly "all up in it." Together, CB and I have five wonderful kids and a beautiful grandchild.

I have my own real estate team, and I have been a recipient of numerous awards. I am excelling in every area of my life, as I could have never imagined. Lord knows that I am receiving many blessings because only what I do for the Lord will last. I am being restored daily; my cup is overflowing, and I am forever giving God all of the Glory and seeking His approval in all that I do!

My life went from being fearful, to remaining faithful, to being restored.

I am Kisha Martin-Burney!

BERSHAN SHAW

Cancer Was My Gift

I wasn't always a warrior; I became one. In March 2007, I heard the worse words of my life—*you have cancer*. It shook me to my core and forever changed my life. After hearing those words, *you have been diagnosed with cancer*, I felt numb like my life had ended. I was single, no kids and I didn't know how I was going to push forward. I left the doctor's office with my paperwork in my hand, and I walked for over fifteen miles. I wandered aimlessly thinking that my life was over. My mother had died of stage 4 breast cancer ten years before and I surely thought I was going to die. Cancer took my mother's life in three months and I was sure it was going to take mine in two.

I was afraid to face my issue and to deal with my disease, so I did what you should never do, which is not tell anyone. I was too embarrassed, and I didn't want to be known as the "sick girl" so I went to radiation and surgery only telling one person—my then-boyfriend. I was ashamed of getting this disease. It was like I had a mark on my life. At that moment the disease was stage 1, and my doctor said to me, "It's like you dodged a bullet." I kept going forward and I didn't want to talk about it or look back. I was thirty-three-years old and I had a life to live.

Two years after the first diagnosis, I had been feeling so much pain in my back that I couldn't move. I couldn't bend down to pick something up off the floor. I had gone to every chiropractor, medical doctor and more to get x-rays and everyone thought it was a slipped disc. I started believing that I had fallen and put my back out of whack, until one day a doctor told me to get an MRI.

I remember the day so clearly, it was a cool spring day in March. I was with my boyfriend and my stepmother. I thought we were stopping by the doctor's office and then we would be off to lunch. I was wrong. When I got to my doctor's office the doctor came into the room with a long white jacket and salt and pepper hair. He didn't say hello, he just said "sit down. I was taken aback. I didn't know why I needed to sit down. He told me that, "I think you need to hear what I have to say. You have been diagnosed with terminal breast cancer." My mouth dropped and hit the floor. I just knew he couldn't be speaking about me. I said, "What did you say?" He said it again, "You have stage 4 breast cancer." I asked him, "What can I do?" "How long do I have?" "What does this mean?" He said, "It's aggressive and you have three to six months to live." I was speechless. It was as if I was lost in time.

When I walked out of the room to have some space and time for myself, I got on my knees and I asked God to use me as a vessel to help others realize that no one can take your life away except Him and if this was my time I'm ready to go. But if it's not, then keep me alive to heal and help people.

I am now eleven years cancer free without any evidence of the disease, and I speak all around the world motivating men and women to help them find their warrior spirit. This was no easy task to get where I am today. I had to change my mindset, my diet, my health, my body and most of all my surroundings. I had to let go of toxic people and stress so that I could heal my body. Below I have come up with a thought process to help you heal and help yourself to be a warrior.

NICOLE S. MASON, ESQUIRE

Identify Your Issues and What's Holding You Back

Ask yourself the hard questions. We often want to run away from our obstacles or difficulties. Secretly we know we eat too much when we are angry, or we have an affair rather than deal with marital difficulties, or shop because we are broke! We've all been there. I have too. We can even use technology to avoid our real feelings. No one wants to admit that, in truth, we hate our jobs, or our relationship has gone dead or that we're flat broke. No one wants to face that we are sick and need to take aggressive action to get well, just when we're not feeling well.

But before we can get into taking action, we have to face what it is that is eating at us or that stops us from sleeping at night and being the best we can be.

A warrior looks his or her "enemy" right straight in the eye. Only then can we find a way to win the battle. You can't win a battle if you're running from it. And by the way, whatever you are ignoring will find you. Problems don't leave town; they stick around till we solve them.

How can you identify your issues? They might be something you don't have the courage to tell your friends or anyone at all. By not speaking, you are hiding the issue from yourself. You are suffering in silence

FAITH FOR FIERY TRIALS

alone when you don't have to. Many people around the world are in the same space as you and you don't realize it. When you are going through a hard time, you shouldn't hide it. You should face it head on. That's the only way to conquer it. Don't give your problems power by letting them control you. If you don't manage them, they will manage you.

Think about a problem you keep talking about over and over, like a broken record, but never do anything about. Talking about a problem is not solving it, nor is worrying constantly. We often forget that. Taking action and doing something about it is dealing with it.

Now is the time to come clean. And be truthful and honest with ourselves about what needs to get better. If we face it, we can solve it. There is always support out there to help us. There is always someone else who has gone through it. We have nothing to be ashamed of. We all face difficulties, we all have strengths and weaknesses.

And we all can make our lives better. But only if we face what is holding us back. Once we face it, we can overcome it and live a fantastic life, basking in our greatness.

Don't Be Afraid of Change and Uncertainty

Facing your challenges with courage means that something inside you and your behavior is going to have to change. If you have financial problems, you're going to have to stop spending or upgrade your income abilities. If your relationship is not working, you are going to have to change your behavior in the relationship or change your partner. If your career isn't working, you are going to have to speak with your boss or change jobs.

Whatever You Are Facing, It Will Require Getting Off Your Butt and Doing Something About It

We are all afraid of change. Can we do it? Can we succeed? Will it be a waste of time? What if it doesn't work out? What if we end up in a worse place?

One reason we may fear change is fear of success. If we've told ourselves a story all our lives, "I can never have abundance," we might not want to prove ourselves wrong by having abundance. We may be frightened of having a boyfriend who is really loving to us, because we have never experienced love as a child and we don't know how to give back in a way we have never seen.

Instead, though, we can look at uncertainty and change as opportunities. Opportunities for things to get better. Opportunities for us to know new parts of ourselves. We can put a positive spin on change. Let's face it, our obstacles and challenges are not the parts of our lives that are going well. So, what have we got to lose? We may really like what we get when we do something new.

And we'll discover strengths we didn't know we had. We may encounter friends and loved ones we might never have met before. We may encounter places we didn't know we would love so intensely.

Change is an opportunity to find our best selves. Carl Jung said, "When we work out of our inferior function, meaning the parts of ourselves that are least developed, we are strengthening the best parts of ourselves at the same time." So, if you hate asking for help, and you finally do it, that new muscle in you will come to play when you least expect it. You might learn a new dance move just because you did something new and you're on a roll now!

So, give up resisting. There is an expression, "Let go or be dragged." We have to give up what is getting in our way. Just let it fall away. That might be the change in itself.

There are no easy answers, life is uncertain. So, accept life's uncertainties as part of being alive. Things always work out the way they are meant to. Life has a way of getting us to where we need to be when we need to be there. Ask yourself:

- Am I willing to change who I am and what I have been?
- Am I okay with being in a state of uncertainty?
- Am I afraid of living life to its fullest?
- Am I willing to do the work on myself?

Communicate Openly and Honestly for Help and Guidance

One significant change we all need to cultivate is asking for help. We can do that in many ways. One is prayer. Even if you don't believe in a divine power, asking and praying for help is a way of telling your subconscious what you need. It's a way of putting it out there for your soul to hear your inner needs, where many answers lie.

To ask for help from people is humbling. You are letting others know you are not invulnerable, that you are human. Everyone needs help at times and, truth is, most people like to help. Most people admire honesty and vulnerability and, by communicating openly and honestly, you are teaching them how to do the same when they need to. Deep down, everyone knows no one gets anywhere all by themselves.

When you ask for help, you are also being loving to yourself. You are taking care of yourself and that may feel strange, at first, but it is progress.

There are lots of answers out there. Where we may be blind on a certain subject, another may be very clear. What has been getting in our way may be the simplest thing to fix for someone else. So, open up and listen to yourself. Go with your gut. Ask, believe and receive. The Universe will send you answers if you *ask, believe and receive.*

If you are consistently dealing with the same thing over and over again, then you need help in that area. It's not the whole of you so don't be ashamed. You will be able to provide help and guidance to others on different subjects. We all have weaknesses where we need the guidance of someone else's eye.

No one is perfect. Great leaders always check with other people. It feels good to talk things out and realize you are not alone. Asking for guidance is a sign of warrior strength. No warrior can win a battle alone. We stand together. Some are good at the front line and some are good in the rear. Some are good at pushing through, some are good at strategizing. But together is how we win a battle. So, turn to others, open up, and let your fellow warriors back you up. They know in their hearts, when the time comes, you will back them up too.

MINISTER BEVERLY LUCAS

Lessons Learned

Cocaine. It was an early Monday morning. I was hallucinating and seeing things I knew were not real. People were floating in the air and cutting their eyes at me. I felt myself feeling as though I had vertigo. Clearly something was wrong. I walked into the office and looked at the secretary and said, "Something is wrong with me." This woman knew me well. We had lived in the same neighborhood and our children grew up together. She did not question what I was saying. She stared at me and said, "Do you want me to call the ambulance." I said, "No. Please call the person on my emergency contact sheet." She looked at the paperwork and said, "Should I call your husband?" I don't know why, but I said, "No." We walked down the stairs and I just started crying. There were no sounds coming from my mouth, but the tears were streaming down uncontrollably. I sat on the stairs as we waited for my ride. The secretary held my hand and prayed for me.

When we arrived at the emergency room, I was still walking in a fog. There were many thoughts going through my mind, but the one thought I could not control was the thought that I was experiencing an Alzheimer's episode. I kept telling myself I was too young, but it was clear my mind was clouded, and my thoughts were mixed.

I have spotty memories of going through the triage. I have intermittent memories of looking my best friend in her eyes and crying. I have glimpses of thinking. I have glimpses of praying. I have many glimpses of that dreadful day. What I do remember and what is crystal clear to me is what substance the doctor said was in my system. He said, "You tested positive for cocaine." I looked at him and replied, "But I don't do cocaine. I have never done cocaine. I have only even seen cocaine once in my life."

Flash Back: We were planning a trip to another country. Things had been very contentious between the two of us, and I was very reluctant to go. I did not want to go. In retrospect, the truth is, I was afraid to go. I remember talking to one of my best friends and I told her that I just did not have a "good" feeling about the trip. I should have listened to myself. I should have followed my gut feeling. I should have trusted my spirit. One night before the trip, I had a dream. In the dream I was deserted on a huge ship that had overturned. Most of the people had jumped overboard, but I was holding on to a pillar and watching people drown. In the dream, an old man showed up, took me by the hand and led me to dry ground. That dream stayed with me for days, but I digress.

We arrived in the country on the Caribbean Sea. Everything was beautiful, bright and breathtaking. The water was crystal clear aqua, and the sand felt as if each grain was the tip of a Q-tip . . . just soft and embracing.

The first night was great. The second day, I was not feeling right. I could not explain it. Perhaps it was the Benadryl because as soon as we arrived, the mosquitos focused on my legs and my legs only. Perhaps it was the variety of tropical drinks. But for some reason, even though I did not have phone service, I messaged my best friend through Facebook a message that said, "I think I am being drugged." She messaged me back alarmed; I felt ashamed I even thought that. I do not know even where there thought came from. I messaged her back that everything was fine and at that moment, everything was fine.

The second day was a nightmare. I was walking around tidying up our room and went to grab a towel off a tall dresser. He looked at me and said, "steady." That was a word he used when he knew I was going to be upset about something. I just ignored him and removed the towel and there were about eight little packets of white powder under the towel. Eight. I counted them. I can be a little naïve, so we both just stood there. He knew it was going to take me a minute to figure it out. "Oh, My God!" My mouth dropped open. "What is this?" "What are you doing?" "You have me in another country with drugs?" "Are you kidding me?" "Did you bring this on the plane?" "Do you know we could be arrested for this?" I couldn't stop with the questions "Why would you do this?" "How long have you been doing this?" "Why would you put your wife in this type of predicament?" He answered no questions. He gave no reply.

I walked away. I went outside to sit on the beach. I got on the Internet searching for a plane ticket to return to America. A one-way ticket for that day was $2,700. I began to strategize on how I was going to get away, but then I remembered. I did not have enough money in my checking account. Okay, I will just transfer money from my savings into the checking, but then I remembered. A few weeks earlier I opened a savings account with a credit union but had never activated my card. Okay, no problem, I will just activate the card. Well, you can't activate a new card in a foreign country.

I stayed out on the beach all day. By the evening, when I entered into the room, the demon was loosed. The man began talking to me in a demonic tone. He told me how stupid I was. He told me I was crazy. He told me I could never tell anyone because they would never believe me. He told me people would never believe anything negative I could say about him, because I had already pumped him up as "the king." He mocked me. He ridiculed me, and then he started to "buck" at me and growled like a dog. The look in his eye was fierce and piercing. The look in his eyes was like the devil himself trying to penetrate through me.

This night, I did all I could do. All I could do was pray. I have never prayed like I prayed that night (and the next night and the next night). I walked around that room and prayed all night. I had my playlist of songs and when I could not pray, I was singing. I sang every song on my playlist: "Take Me to the King," "Nobody Like You Lord," "Giants Do Fall" "Awesome God," "A Song of Strength," "Give me a Clean Heart," "Praise Him in Advance," and the list goes on and on. The longer I prayed and sang, the less strength the demon showed. Eventually, he was all out of strength. The morning came.

The next day, I told him that my spirit was too strong for him and that he was never going to "break me" (that is what the demon said). I told him that it was never going to work. I told him that he knew me then he should have known that none of this behavior was ever going to work for us. We had a good day that day. It was always "good" (relatively) before there was any mind-altering usage, but when the evening arrived, it became a vicious cycle. I literally did not sleep for three nights. I stayed up all night and slept during the day on the beach. I was afraid of what would happen if I closed my eyes in that room. By day five, I had prayed so much, I had absolutely no fear. I felt like the Holy Spirit was all over me. There was nothing he could do or say that could shake me. I knew that I was going to return to the United States of America!

The Lord made several things clear to me. Yes, I loved this man and yes, this man loved me. But his problems were beyond my scope of understanding. The problems he had were beyond the realm of my control. This level of behavior did not happen overnight. It was a slow, progressive and manipulative process. The problem with me was, I let it ride. The problem with me was, I let down my guard in certain areas that should always be covered. The problem with me was, I was so in love, I missed the signs. Some signs I missed, others I ignored.

Embarrassment, disappointment and disbelief held me captive. The more bizarre the behavior evolved, the more secluded I became. I made excuses for my children not to come to the house. I stopped having my granddaughter over because I could not even bare the chance of her innocence witnessing and listening to someone belittling her Nana. My heart trembles at that thought!

One night, out of anger, he finally grabbed me. That was the last night we were together. I promised him that if he ever touched me to harm me, that would be the end. I slept in my car that night and the next night. It is not that I did not have anywhere to go. It is not that I could not have called anyone of my friends or relatives. It is not that I was homeless. Again, embarrassment, disappointment and disbelief held me captive. I needed to figure out what to do next and more importantly, how to do it. Finally, I checked into a hotel and the process of my grief and depression began.

I had to go through countless sessions of therapy to begin the healing process. But thank God, I was willing to do the work. Every day is a new day. Every day I am willing and enthusiastically doing the work. I have learned that healing can only take place when you are committed to and discover the truth of who you are. As I am discovering my truth, the world has opened; it is like a rosebud blossom. My personal life, blossoms. My professional life blossoms and my educational pursuits blossom. It is like my world is blossoming. The first book I authored is entitled, *Blossom: A Christian Woman's Journey of Self-Discovery*. My life has come full circle. I am embracing what I have always been advocating.

In all this mess (and as you can imagine, this story is only a tip of the iceberg), I can say, I never lost faith, hope or trust in God. My faith was fortified. My hope was renewed, and my trust was completely in Him. I have shared bits and pieces; I am sure you can connect the dots.

I share this story because I know it can help someone who is in a situation that you never imagined could happen to you. Yes, God will give you a strategy. You are never stuck. I share this story because secrets are too heavy to carry. I share this story because it is my truth. This is my narrative of what happened to me. I found out from sitting out on a beach at midnight that life is surely like a vapor. I found out from sitting out on a beach that no matter what situation I may find myself in, God is omnipresent. I found out from sitting on a beach that I had unshakable faith for fiery trials!

ELDER ANGELA MINOR, ESQUIRE

Grieving in Truth

Grief can be a weapon. Albeit, a necessary and natural emotion in every human being. Grief can become a weapon that can change the course of your life in the absence of truth. Grief can consume your heart and your mind. When you are in a place of grief, it is akin to being on a merry-go-round, but refusing to jump off. Grief is a cyclic force, as it is characterized by the recurrence of pain that runs throughout your thinking. Grief and pain can often be in opposition with your faith and belief. The consistency of the pain of losing a loved one is strong enough to cause an individual, even a believer, to surrender to a lifestyle of living in grief. The knowledge of what grief does when it presents itself and takes up residence in your heart can only be revealed through a relationship with Jesus Christ.

When you chase Christ while you are grieving, expect a full recovery!

Cancer was the diagnosis, a rare form of stomach cancer when my beloved mother checked into the hospital for what was supposed to be a simple hysterectomy. When first diagnosed, the cancer was in one primary location in her body. Fortunately, at that point, it was not metastatic cancer (it had not spread to other parts of her body). This was the first time I experienced the death of a loved one that was a part of my immediate family. Being saved has its benefits, but until you let Christ deliver you from your deepest and darkest places of hurt, you will be consumed with grief and unable to mature to your full potential.

Grieving in truth is your ability to trust God to heal you in the stages of your pain. It is viewing grief as a divine mechanism that will further your relationship with God. Grief can be a divine action. It is a tool that God can use to heal you, shape you and consecrate you. Grieving is a mental state that causes you to bare your soul, as death is so shocking and emotionally painful that it subdues anyone in its path. Once you are confronted with grief and pain, it can humble you before the Lord and cause you to instantly chase Him. You begin to chase God while you chase your pain. Dealing with the death of my mother exposed me to a new level of vulnerability before the Lord. The feeling of helplessness ad loneliness was a constant space. When the surgery doesn't help and the chemotherapy doesn't help, you feel helpless. When you are praying, but your circumstances do not change, you feel helpless. Helplessness is so prevalent because we are busy living our lives and nothing can prepare you for an unexpected, untimely death.

Grief is not initially understood or viewed as a divine mechanism. When you are experiencing the tragedy of losing a parent quickly, you are incapable of always seeing the purpose in your pain. Tragedy is dramatic and overwhelming. Cancer is the type of parasite or illness that causes your loved one to deteriorate before your very eyes.

My mother lost her energy, her hair, and her weight in a matter of weeks. My father and I were there to the very end until she took her last breath in the hospital. Being an only child, this was a very devastating time in my life. I couldn't see why God needed to pull me closer to Him during my mother's illness. I wanted to pull away from God. I witnessed my mother experience so much pain until she couldn't talk; the suffering of this disease was unbearable to watch.

How do you focus on the love of Christ while you are witnessing the suffering of the one who Christ used to display His love on earth to you? I had to relearn that the power of love will never fail you. Love is graceful, but it requires the heart to forgive and live through any pain or obstacle. My mother's love was admirable including her voice, her touch, her actions and her ability to see the very best in everyone around her. "Love is patient; love is kind. It does not envy; it does not boast, it is not proud. It is not rude; it is not self-seeking, it is not easily angered, it keeps no record of wrongs. Love does not delight in evil but rejoices with the truth. It always protects, always trusts, always hopes, always perseveres." (I Corinthians 13:4-8 NIV) I have never experienced a love like my mother's love, and I'm sure I never will!

My mother never gave me hopelessness, despair, manipulation or pain beyond repair. I had the most beautiful relationship a mother and daughter could experience. I had the type of mother who was totally 100% invested in my wellbeing. I often agonized and cried out to the Lord asking, "Why her? Why my mother? Why the one whose love was so important to me?" At that time, I could only see my pain. The ability to let go of the flesh and function or move in the spirit of faith on a consistent basis should be a daily goal.

The Lord showed me that my pain could never lead me to a place of wholeness and peace. Love is far from pain. Pain causes some to ignore the love in our heart. I learned that love is a place of perseverance during this experience. Perseverance simply means, "A steady persistence in a course of action, a purpose, a state; especially in spite of difficulties, obstacles or discouragement." One preferred theological definition of perseverance is, "The continuance of being in a state of grace to the end, leading to eternal salvation." I wanted to believe God would heal her because we are taught that, "He is a miracle working God!" I had to drop the religiousness and become a God chaser, and grace covered me every step of the way.

God is sovereign! Become vulnerable and openly submissive to the Lord's sovereignty. For instance, under the pain of losing my mother, I cried, yelled, stomped, complained, cussed, moaned and rebelled at the truth! My pain was all that I wanted to see. When I realized I couldn't live in depression, couldn't live sleeping in bed hours at a time, couldn't live holding in my emotions and masking my feelings, I began crying out to God, more and more. I was ready to begin to grieve in truth. Grieving in truth is giving the process over to the Lord. Nothing satisfied me like the peace of my Lord and Savior, Jesus Christ! I said nothing filled me like God's grace, mercy and peace.

Jesus grieved, and Jesus wept! "And the Lord was sorry He had made man on the earth, and He was grieved in His heart." (Genesis 6:6 NKJV) It grieved

God's heart when Adam and Eve fell victim to sin in the Garden of Eden. Secondly, Isaiah 53:3, "Jesus is a man of sorrows and acquainted with grief and that He has born our grief and carries our sorrows." Also, Ephesians 4:30 states, "And do not grieve the Holy Spirit of God, by whom you were sealed for the day of redemption." The Bible tells us that our sin grieves the Holy Spirit, yet we will also have the saving grace of our Lord and Savior through Jesus Christ. Furthermore, He has left us His spirit, the Holy Spirit, our Comforter. Therefore, Jesus grieves. He grieves with us, because His spirit abides within us.

Some scholars have compartmentalized grief into many stages: shock and denial, pain and guilt, anger and bargaining; depression and reflection; and finally, loneliness. (See www.recoverfromgrief.com) There is no specific order for emotional grieving. It is experienced on a case-by-case basis. However, when your grief surrenders to the move of the Holy Spirit; you are working in a place of balance and peace.

Otherwise, grieving without God causes pain to be exacerbated which leads to an exhausting pattern of emotional turmoil. Emotions pull you around and around, wherein, you are unable to see or think straight. When you voluntarily ride a merry-go-round, you know what to expect; it's movement is familiar. When you are grieving the loss of a family member, you have no idea what's ahead. Your life has been altered forever and will never be the same.

Grieving with God is not easy, but it's worth it. The depth of pain is no match for your omnipotent God. God gave me time to heal from pain, grief and depression. God had a plan for my process. The process of your grief is what the Lord wants you to surrender to Him, so He can begin to heal you as you are still coping with pain. First, the Lord showed me how to recognize my grief. Awareness of self was the first stage of my healing. For example, your grief may be too much sleeping, isolating yourself from people— staying at home, letting go of attending church, or over-working. I began to recognize things that I did not see in myself prior to my mother's passing. Holding in your pain causes the physical manifestation of hurt to be visible in your appearance. I am reminded of the scripture, "So as a man thinketh in his heart, so is he." (Proverbs 23:7 KJV)

Additionally, I had to stop looking down all the time. My behavior and looks began to mimic my pain. God had to expose the pain that was over my physical appearance. All of a sudden, strangers in coffee shops and public places would ask me, "Why do you look so sad?" or "Are you okay?" Immediately, I developed an awareness of who I was becoming because the Lord used those people to show me what I looked like on the outside. Everything I was spiritually connected to could not prosper because my pain was over it. Spiritual pain, in palliative care, understanding and managing emotional or spiritual pain is as important as managing physical pain. We know from speaking to people living with a terminal illness, and their families and friends, that emotional or spiritual pain is common regardless of religion, beliefs or culture. (See www.mariecurie.org). My pain affected my anointing. My pain affected my ability to praise and pray. God revealed the truth about me in a manner that made me uncomfortable. I was naïve to think that no one could see my pain.

I started to reject the pain that I chose to carry and accept the healing that was ahead. Acceptance was my second stage of healing. Simply put, healing was accepting the truth. Accepting the truth, that I could never hold, touch, see my mother in the physical sense ever again. I have learned that I can do all those things by God's spirit as He gives me dreams, glimpses of our time together and brings precious memories of my mother to the forefront of my mind in His way and in His timing. I have acknowledged the truth by grieving in a way that God gets the glory! Never consider yourself alone after losing a loved one.

FAITH FOR FIERY TRIALS

God gets the glory when you tell your story. Tell your story in church, on the job (when permissible) and at events with friends and to family members. The reciprocal award of sharing your grief with others is accepting that pain exists but can be controlled by your faith in Jesus Christ. Your pain does have a purpose, and the reward is helping another person heal just like Christ helped me heal. Have faith in Jesus. Have faith that He understands your grief, can help you control your grief and can give you ways to escape the understanding that binds or hinders your ability to move forward in your walk with the Lord. 1 Corinthians 10:13 states, "No temptation has overtaken you except such as is common to man; but God is faithful, who will not allow you to be tempted beyond what you are able, but with the temptation will also make the way of escape, that you may be able to bear it." (NKJV)

Understanding the truth of my reality was greater than the pain I found myself in. Once you understand that acceptance is the opposite of denial when you are grieving, you can build your strength in the knowledge of God's Word. The Bible is wisdom that God will use to strengthen your inability to move forward. Denial is the refusal to move forward. I was in denial that my mother was dying before my eyes and subsequently, could not accept her death until the day of her passing. Then, I transferred my denial to anger against God. I asked God, "How could you let this happen?" Then, I moved to a place of anger towards God. I knew not to question God. So, when I did question God, I had deep regret and conviction.

I began to regret not being there for her. I regretted that I was not there for every single chemotherapy treatment or every time she got sick when I was working in the District of Columbia, and she was living with my father in Virginia. I wanted to do anything to change the circumstances. I blamed myself. My scapegoat became emotionalism. I also knew that I couldn't leave God and walk away from the One who had been my source of strength over the course of my life. I was so angry through that I removed myself from the spirit of truth. What I mean by *leaving God* is withdrawing to a place of fear and pain. I praise God that He called me unto righteousness once again by showing me that His love was greater than any pain I could ever feel.

The love of God is so amazing and words cannot describe it! In my healing, I began to have visions of my mother, and I remember her in ways I didn't know I had stored in the back of my mind or my heart. The connection I had with God linked me to the spirit of healing which opened doors for me to accept what my mother left with me. My mother always proclaimed,

"Your darkest hour is just before dawn." She left me with a business, a heart of joy, a cadre of people who knew her and loved her, friends and family.

I'm able to embody her grace, virtue and love as her DDD (Dearest Darling Daughter), which is what she affectionately called me and spread that joy to all those who were impacted by her life. Accepting to grieve in truth employs you as an agent for Christ. Christ can use me to reach other individuals who grieved like I did. I grieved with more emotional pain than spiritual guidance for years. Now, I am equipped with knowledge, truth and understanding to grieve in truth.

The revelation knowledge of grieving in truth and the wisdom of God is now over my life. I have accepted my pain as a divine mechanism that God used to remove hate, poor health conditions, and lack of faith. My mother's passing has brought me closer to God than I ever could have imagined. No more uncontrollable pain or a heart that doesn't waver to acknowledge the truth over hurt in all circumstances. God is able to take you from pain to gain!

The gain I'm speaking of is hope! God moves in the spirit of truth and healing over your pain. Hope is your measure of faith that carries you and establishes you to witness in truth. Having hope is the kind of optimistic behavior that leads you to the light of Jesus

Christ and out of suffering in darkness. The Lord will keep you no matter how emotionally deep your pain runs. God is so beautifully patient, loving and kind. Experiencing the loss of a loved one that was such a huge part of your life requires you to allow the Lord to possess that vacant territory in your heart. There is no one who could take the place of your loved one. God will call you to a deeper level of understanding in Him. He will establish your thinking and repossess your pain. The pain will always resurface, but God will show you how to manage your grief in truth. When I gave my pain over to the Lord, my anxiety, my inability to get out of the bed and depression could no longer bind me.

My value had existed so heavily in my mother's validation. Your parents are the first people to validate you, support you and love you. I had an extremely close relationship with my mother. She was everything to me. My best friend and my business partner. We owned a law firm together. Then, the unimaginable happened—her death. So that there is no confusion, I knew how to live my life for Christ. I also knew that I was my own person. What I didn't know was how to live without someone, my mother, who gave me a strong support system. Mothers are unique. We are fortunate to have good mothers in our lives. Mothers who know how to follow what Proverbs 22:6 says,

"Train up a child in the way he should go, And when he is old he will not depart from it." I had a mom like that; a mother that put God first in her life and made sure that I put Him first in mine.

In coping in truth and strength, I have hope that can withstand the deepest and darkest circumstances. HOPE is an acronym for Having Onward Power to Embrace! I'm moving forward with my life. My process changed when God showed me how to get off the merry-go-round of pain!

Remember to let the Lord give you:

1. Awareness of self (see the truth)
2. Acceptance, not denial (accept the truth)
3. Hope and deliverance! Deliverance is a daily journey to embrace humbly!

I bid you God's speed.

Sandra,
Keep the faith!
Trust God! ♡

Tracey
xx

TRACEY SIMMS WASHINGTON

The Faith and Grace of a Warrior

I smiled the first time that I intentionally said to myself in the mirror, "I love you Tracey, and I am so proud of you." Within seconds, I began to adore every inch of me. I felt a huge transformation taking place inside of me mentally, spiritually and psychologically. All the years of hard work on myself has finally come to fruition. No more chains to my past, low self-esteem, unworthiness, and reckless relationships. I am not attached to my past as a victim anymore, but my past is divinely connected to my victory.

As a celebrated empty nester, I have many loving, empowering, and sometimes comical conversations with myself. Those days I pass by the mirror, and I am looking good and feeling good, I say, "Harpo, Who that woman?" I crack myself up sometimes. It has become easier not to take myself and other people so seriously now. They say laughter is good for the soul, and I am so thankful that all is well with my soul. Joy and laughter are huge contributors to the healing process of my recent cancer diagnosis and the recovery from severe depression and low self-esteem.

I heard someone say, a stress-free life is a happy life. But nobody's life is entirely stress-free; however, we have to care enough about ourselves to manage the stress in our lives responsibly. It is a fact that too much stress, anger, unforgiveness, and over-extended grief can lead us to a multitude of physical and mental health challenges. So, we have to speak kind words to ourselves and refrain from speaking negatively about others. Until now, I didn't know how to digest the hurtful words and actions that were directed towards me; so, I unconsciously internalized them.

After a while, I began to speak negatively to myself. Words are powerful; those that we say to ourselves and those that we say about others. Some people, like me, are natural encouragers. We can effortlessly speak life into others, but we neglect to do the same for ourselves. Words can either lift us up or tear us down, whether they come out of our mouths or remain under our breath marinating in our spirit.

Proverbs 18:21 says, "The tongue can bring death or life; those who love to talk will reap the consequences." (NLT) The translation of this scripture cannot be more straightforward than that.

I am blessed that life has brought me to this place of healing, self-love and self- empowerment. I dance for joy at the transformation. I beam at the thought of my continual elevation. For everyone and everything that is responsible for who I see in the mirror today, I thank you. I am at peace with my past and excited about my future. This joy that I have is a direct result of the triumphs, trials, and tribulations of my life. In an interview, Oprah Winfrey referred to an old Negro Spiritual, "Wouldn't Take Nothin' for my Journey Now." I agree with Oprah. I never saw my tumultuous journey coming. But when I look back over my life, and I think things over, I can truly say that I am blessed, and I have a testimony. So, come on in the room as I share with you my amazing grace and increasing faith journey.

For many years, I tried to figure out my life's purpose on my own. Then I prayed for God to reveal His purpose for my life and God responded. I learned that my purpose was in my story: the good, the bad and the ugly. I knew my life was full of lessons learned, but sharing my flaws scared me and I sat on it for a while. I ran from the thought of using my life story to help others, but then one day, it all made perfect sense. I kept praying, and it seemed like God laid it out for me clearly when I heard Dr. Tony Evans preach on the Book of Esther.

I had studied the story of Esther before, and I thought that my life led a similar path. Esther was admired for her beauty, and I am always complimented on my looks. Esther took responsibility for saving the lives of her family, and I have helped my family since I was a teen with various life situations. God continued to use Dr. Evans' message when he said, "God blesses you to use you for something bigger. You have been put here for something bigger, and if you lose the bigger, you lose the purpose. God delivered you and has set you free, he expects you to deliver somebody else." That is a powerful charge to everyone! Esther was afraid to speak to the king to save the Jews from death. God is never mentioned in the book of Esther. However, God used Mordecai to clarify to Esther the importance of why she was called to speak to the king. In Esther 4:13–17 Mordecai sent this reply to Esther: "Don't think for a moment that because you're in the palace you will escape when all other Jews are killed. If you keep quiet at a time like this, deliverance and relief for the Jews will arise from some other place, but you and your relatives will die. Who knows if perhaps you were made queen for just such a time as this?" Then Esther sent this reply to Mordecai: "Go and gather together all the Jews of Susa and fast for me. Do not eat or drink for three days, night or day. My maids and I will do the same. And then, though it is against the law, I will go in to see the king. If I must die, I must die." So, Mordecai went away and did everything as Esther had ordered him. (NLT)

Dr. Evans said, "With anything in life, you will take a risk. So, take a risk on God." Just like Esther, I am taking a risk on God; being obedient to the calling on my life to turn my mess into a message with a purpose. With all that I have been through in my life, God has given me this platform to use my story to uplift His Kingdom. Esther's dilemma pertained to her life and the lives of the Jews. My dilemma, do I ignore my God-ordained purpose or make the sacrifice, and put all my business out there to help others? Just like Esther, the tone has been set by God to do His will. I have no worries about what people say about me anymore. I have repented, I am forgiven, I forgive myself, and I am covered by the blood of Jesus. No one can tell my story better than me anyway.

When I was born, my Mama said that she and her girlfriends chose my names, Tracey Lynette. When I learned that my name Tracey means brave and warrior, I had to dig deeper for more information. I was born in 1968, and according to Wikipedia, "the name Tracey was the sixth most popular female name in the 1960s and is taken from the Irish word "treasach" meaning "war-like or fighter." It is also translated as "higher," "more powerful" or "superior." My middle name Lynette, according to the Urban dictionary means, "A girl that is tough but pretty at the same time. She can be your best friend if you show her respect, but your greatest nightmare if you don't! She has an amazing personality but can also be quiet at times. You have to get to know Lynette to see how amazing she is." So that explains it. The spirit of God moved mightily in my Mama and her friends, and I am thankful that they listened.

God has seen me through all the conflicts that eventually worked out in my favor. "I am fearfully and wonderfully made" comes to my mind, but I love the powerful version of Psalm 139: 14-16 (The Message Bible) that says, "Oh yes, you shaped me first inside, then out; you formed me in my mother's womb. I thank you, Most High God—you're breathtaking! Body and soul, I am marvelously made! I worship in adoration—what a creation! You know me inside and out, you know every bone in my body; You know exactly how I was made, bit by bit, how I was sculpted from nothing into something. Like an open book, you watched me grow from conception to birth; all the stages of my life were spread out before you, The days of my life all prepared before I'd even lived one day."

When I read the Message version of this scripture, my spirit jumped, my shoulders pulled back and my head lifted, the same way that I felt in the mirror that day. I hope you felt it, too. I am somebody special because God made me that way. Who can argue with that, right? Wrong, I used to argue about it all the time. I would judge myself and others, and then get in my feelings when someone judged me. Until we believe God, trust God, and take Him at His Word, it is very difficult to not argue with these powerful words about how God created and sustains us.

So, how did I get here? How did I get to a place of surrender to what God says about me, instead of what my enemies said to me and about me? How did I survive being single most of my adult life, when my dream was to be married with four kids, and at least one set of twins? How did I not commit suicide when I felt like the walls were closing in and I could not breathe? What about all the mean and destructive things that they did to me? How in the world could I have peace and joy while fighting this monstrous Leiomyosarcoma cancer and these chemotherapy treatments? How can I be so sure that God will heal me from this disease and allow me to fulfill my life's purpose?

My answer: *He did it before, and He will do it again*! My answer is more than just a cliché; look at what He has already done for me:

- God restored me from the trauma of rape, divorce, abortion, being arrested in front of my child, and standing in an arraignment line up.
- God healed me from the trauma and pain of emotional, narcissistic, physical, spiritual and verbal abuse; public humiliation, post-traumatic stress disorder, depression, spinal stenosis, and endometriosis.
- God delivered me from grieving my Daddy's death, thoughts of suicide, surrendering to unavailable men, family dysfunction, low self-esteem, loneliness, codependency, childhood/adult bullying, rejection, fear of failure and success.

Okay, now breathe everybody! I am sure my transparency is much easier for me to share than it is for you to absorb all at once like this; especially if you know me personally. But that's okay because I have already lifted you in prayer to appreciate my story in the spirit of testimony and the resurrecting power of Jesus Christ. This is my testimony. This is why I still have joy in spite of all that I am going through now. God restored, healed and delivered me through it all. I am still here, standing strong and proud of what God has done through me and in me.

So, can a diagnosis of cancer or anything else have any power over me now? My answer is *absolutely not*! Why? Because my fight against Uterine Leiomyosarcoma cancer has been somewhat of a Godsent blessing in disguise. Let me explain. A cancer diagnosis is an extremely shocking and traumatic medical diagnosis. For me, the diagnosis was not confirmed right away, so instead of surrendering to the possibility of Leiomyosarcoma cancer written on my MRI report, I began researching every word on my MRI report and implementing every anecdote to prevent a confirmed diagnosis of cancer. After a full hysterectomy, the cancer diagnosis was confirmed. But that's not the end of the story, so let me tell you about God's perfect timing. I was prepared for this.

Remember, I am restored, healed and delivered from all those experiences. So, a year before my diagnosis, God revealed to me, through my counseling and self-empowerment work, that many of my life's struggles were due to being overly empathetic and codependent. According to *Psychology Today*,

"Empathy is the experience of understanding another person's thoughts, feelings, and condition from their point of view, rather than from your own. You try to imagine yourself in their place in order to understand what they are feeling or experiencing." *Mental Health America* says that, "Codependency is an emotional and behavioral condition that affects an individual's ability to have a healthy, mutually satisfying relationship. It is also known as "relationship addiction" because people with codependency often form or maintain relationships that are one-sided, emotionally destructive and/or abusive." I realized that I was the common denominator in so many unhealthy relationships and friendships; I had to fight for my freedom. I prayed. I did the work, and I praised God for every small victory. Have faith and trust in God, then stop, look and listen before you cross the road leading to the desires of your heart.

Stop – Know when it is time to just be still and only talk to God - *Pray*

Look – Observe all the resources that God will put in your path to help you – *Do the work*

Listen– Receive God's voice and go walk in your greatness – *Praise Him*

Let us pray, "Father God, Thank You for Your son, Jesus Christ, who sacrificed His perfect life for our imperfections, and rose again for our salvation. Thank You for Your grace and mercy allowing the amazing visionary and co-authors to share their fiery trials as a testimony of Your faithfulness and grace to be servants in Your Kingdom. Lord, thank You for all of the many readers of this book.

We pray that through the testimonies and the transparency of each author, many prayers will be answered, and many lives will be changed forever.

Lord, we pray that if anyone reading this book does not know Jesus Christ as their personal Lord and Savior, we pray that, *Faith for Fiery Trials* will be a sacred and anointed resource that many will want to know, "What must I do to be saved, restored, healed, and delivered, too?"

Lord, we thank You in advance for all that is manifested through each person involved, connected, and all who will contribute to the success of this book collaboration experience.

Lord, when it is evident that our prayers are answered according to Your Will; we promise to give You all the glory, honor and praise in the name of Jesus, Amen."

MINISTER MARY HARRIS

Burnt but Blessed

Have you ever looked in the mirror and didn't recognize the face staring back at you? Have you stared at the eyes reflecting the pain and brokenness that life heaped on your poor soul; looking as if a doomsday bomb detonated in your soul shattering the very core of who you were into millions of scattered pieces? That poor soul was me! I had hit after hit from birth to the point of my crumbling marriage. I was tired of fighting everything a woman could have thrown at her. I didn't want to be the poster child for anything that could happen to a woman! As far as I was concerned, enough was truly enough.

Have you ever been sucker punched by life? Well, that's exactly how I felt. I remember looking at myself in the bathroom mirror and not recognizing the woman staring back at me. I had already attempted suicide by walking in front of an eighteen-wheeler as my estranged husband listened to my ravings so that he could hear how far the devastation his decisions had pushed me. I had considered homicide because I rationalized it was easier to be a widow rather than a divorcee. Crazy, Right? I begged him to return home with no regard for my dignity or self-respect. I compromised my integrity and allowed myself to be relegated to the mistress, not my God-given role of wife. I had cried, screamed, and cussed to the point of exhaustion. In the darkness of those moments, dark voices plagued my mind with negativity. I was losing my mind. The depth of my pain was so palpable, deep and unwavering in its intensity that I physically felt hurt. I was broken, depressed and oppressed.

Why? Why had God abandoned me at my most vulnerable? Didn't He promise never to leave or forsake me? I had done all I could do to be that Proverbs 31 chick. You know the image of pure, perfected womanhood. I was sold out for Christ, active in church, successful at work, and holding it down as a mother and wife. I wasn't perfect, but I was obedient to God's Word. Didn't God care about my pain? After all, He was my Father and Creator! Why didn't I get a vision or sign that my happily ever after was going to turn into hell on earth? God was silent! I was angry at the One who I was always able to count on. He was there with me before I was even conscious of who He was and who I was in Him.

As in the Langston Hughes poem entitled, "Mother to Son" that reads, "Life for me ain't been no crystal stair," I was a child born of a married man's indiscretion with a sixteen-year-old girl who was rebelling against everything and everyone who cared about her. My mother didn't want me; still a child herself, she only wanted to flush her problem down the toilet. But my grandmother, affectionately called Mom Mary, wasn't having it. She got my mom to the hospital, and I came into this world screaming at the top of my lungs. A child already labeled by this world as a bastard before it was politically incorrect to say such things. Before I was a week old, I was taken by my mom and left with a kind, but complete stranger's family. In that home, I was wrapped up in a blanket covering my head by the stranger's younger sister who saw me as a living baby doll; but God spared my life and guided my dad against all odds to find me.

He returned this hungry, swollen-faced, tearful infant to my grandparents where I was raised in the church and learned to love the Lord with my whole heart. But the devil was still coming for me. From the day I accepted Christ at six years of age through adulthood, he came for me through molestation to multiple rapes, promiscuity, cancer, welfare, single parenthood, domestic violence, suicide attempts and low self-esteem. God continued to protect, keep and restore me. He was with me in the darkest places in my life. I finally rededicated myself to Christ in 2001 at Greater Mount Calvary Holy Church's Annual New Year's Revival. I was sold out for Christ! So why now after surviving all of that was God leaving me out in the deep alone? I was sinking in an ocean of pain. I needed to hear God answer my cries in my midnight hour.

At this point, I stopped talking. I no longer had the strength to argue with God nor my estranged husband. I can hear you saying, "You argued with God!" Yes, I came unapologetically before God naked in my hurt, anger and pain; and I did not get a reply. I no longer wanted to fight for a marriage that only I appeared to want. I did everything I could to save my marriage as a good, godly wife who believed in her covenant commitment to God and my husband.

I forgave infidelity, went to therapy and pastoral counseling, fasted, prayed and compromised my integrity and self-respect to no avail. After weeks of inquiries on where my husband was and the shame that accompanies the secret of a failing marriage, I had had enough of going to church, too. I started to isolate myself from everyone and everything that loved me and gave me joy. I was tired, in pain and very lost. Sometimes you have to hit rock bottom to realize where you are because you can't stay there anymore. I was still and had no movement! I was afraid of going forward and unable to go backward because nothing was there for me. I had become comfortable in my uncomfortableness.

Have you ever wanted to move past your pain but didn't know how to do so? I couldn't see my way out, but I started to feel it was time to let go of my estranged husband, the heartbreak and the sorrow of lost dreams. When a marriage dies, so does all the hopes, dreams and goals that accompanies it. If you talk to any therapist, you'll find it is the same feeling as in the death of a loved one. You go through the same five stages of grief (denial, anger, bargaining, depression, and acceptance) in no particular order. I felt all those stages as I walked through the almost three years of separation except for the stage of acceptance. When you're in the dark, you can't see the light, but you know the light is there somewhere. I couldn't accept the fact that I wouldn't grow old with him. We wouldn't share the many years to come together. He wanted marriage, but not marriage with me.

Although I was still emotionally broken, dejected and ashamed, I returned to my church which was my solace and place of healing. Although I hadn't talked to God in a while, He was working behind the scene to manifest a breakthrough. Every Sunday my pastors: Archbishop Alfred Owens, Jr., Co-Pastor Susie Owens and Bishop T. Cedric Brown preached sermons that spoke to my pain, but even more so, my healing. God was talking again or I was listening again; either way, those sermons started to chip away at my frozen heart. The Holy Spirit was doing surgery on my heart getting out all the infection which was eating away at me. I felt the Holy Spirit envelop me with consuming peace.

As if answering a prayer yet spoken, the sisterhood of women in my church and at work shared their stories and gave their support on a scale I have never experienced in my life. I was surrounded by a wall of love and support from women despite dealing with their own marital hells. The transparency of those amazing women coupled with the sense I no longer was alone was within itself, overwhelming, yet empowering. Words can't adequately describe the full meaning of all it meant to me to have someone who knew exactly what I was going through. We had a reciprocal relationship with a glance, knowing through smiles and hugs, we understood each other's pain and comforted each other. As Elder Nicole Mason says, "There's power in the ministry of presence." The ability to discern when someone is in emotional pain and simply needs you to be present without saying a word, yet speaking volumes, was a phenomenon only God could have orchestrated. These women poured oil into my almost empty vessel like Ruth filled up Naomi's heart, so she was no longer called bitter in the Book of Ruth. God used these women to reach back for me in my despair and pray me, push me and pull me through the flames that threatened to consume me.

On March 20, 2014, a day before my birthday, my divorce was finalized within ten minutes. I walked out of that courthouse in a daze to the subway station as tears silently rolled down my face. As I entered the subway car, out of my peripheral vision, I saw my now ex-husband board the same train. I placed my earphone in my ears and pressed play on my phone and Mary J. Blige belted out, "Not Gonna Cry." I couldn't do anything but let the tears flow. I kept looking at the Divorce Decree trying to take in the finality of the words on the pages and it seemed the words "Dissolution of Marriage" jumped off the page. My marriage was dissolved for eighty dollars and in ten minutes. I could see in my mind's eye all the moments of laughter, love and support. I could feel his kiss on our wedding day. I also could see our last moment as husband and wife at the funeral of his beloved grandmother who meant the world to me. We held hands and comforted each other. It was just a month before our final appearance to finalize our divorce. It was, in a sense, a gift because the man I loved reemerged one last time. I was able to be with my in-loves one last time as his wife and a member of their loving family who had embraced my kids and me. As I snapped out of the vivid memories of my lost life, I had enough nerve to look in his direction, and I saw him wipe tears from his eyes, too.

After several years of separation and now divorced, I was slowly healing, but not entirely accepting the reality of being divorced. My ex-husband had moved on long before the ink had dried on the Divorce Decree. I was sitting on the couch in my therapist's office reiterating the consistent feelings of anger and filling stuck. During a pivotal point in my healing, my therapist who was a clinical professional as well as a Christian said, "You are right where you should be emotionally. It's normal! You are precious to God, and your Father won't give you to just anyone." She started to outline all my pluses. It was if a lightbulb came on in my head! I was worth more than being someone else's second best. I started to reclaim my life, bit by bit and day by day. My ex-husband left me with a self-fulfilling prophecy when he said, "Mary, you may not see it now, but this is the best thing for you." Today, I can say he was so right! Initially, I couldn't see past my pain because the intensity of the loss of my marriage in such a truly unexpected manner knocked me off my axis. He was my best friend, my confidant, my lover and my rock, so I didn't see it coming and never at the depth of betrayal I experienced. But God! He propelled my past beyond my pain to my purpose.

You can't always see in the valley of despair the mountain of destiny that you are climbing. No one could have told me I would make it through all the things I have overcome. Just like in the Book of Job, I've been tested! This has been a Job experience. Like me, I know many of you can't fully see your mountain top because you are too far down in the valley of whatever you are facing; be it divorce, health issues, loss of a loved one or loss of employment. But I promise you, God is in the valley, the fiery furnace, the dark tunnel or whatever you call your current situation with you. In the Book of Job, God suggested to Satan the consideration of Job because God knew what Satan didn't. Job was equipped for the lot that would befall him.

Know that God equipped you, too! Like me, one day you will see the lessons and blessings of your valley experience. I discovered with God; I will never fail. I may be temporarily blocked or stopped, but never defeated! I also see my divorce and all that it entailed as a delivery room where God fully birthed my divine destiny and purpose in Christ. Our most difficult, seemingly hopeless situations are merely delivery rooms where God is perfecting and birthing within us things that we have been carrying way too long.

I also discovered I must truly love the woman in the mirror who is staring back at me before I can expect someone else to love her. Now I fully and completely love and value myself. I am the King's daughter, and He doesn't give His daughter to just anybody. You and I are royalty! Even when I didn't see God's hands, He was orchestrating my healing and deliverance. The worst events in our lives are most often the birth places of our purpose.

When walking through the fires of life, you don't always feel like you'll make it out alive. Not only will you come out, but you'll be better for the journey. Someone is reading this who doesn't feel they'll ever be alright. You've accepted pain as your permanent zip code. But God is saying, not so! Like me, you think what you're losing is the end of your world, but it's the beginning of the fulfillment of God's calling. It was for me! Out of my pain came purpose for my good and God's glory.

Repeatedly, God didn't let me die in any of the many traps the enemy set for me. What the enemy meant for my evil, God turned it all around for my good. In the midst of life's most difficult moments, there is always a glimmer of light that urges us to go on. That light encourages us to push through the pain, disappointment, and hurt of life to grab hold of hope and possibilities for the better. It is these moments of darkness that truly define who we are or choose to become. Choose to not just survive life's difficulties but emerge like the Phoenix thriving in the midst of the fires of adversity and soaring higher.

CHERYL MERCER

Losing Erin

"Mom, can you do my hair for me, just a few curls?" I was exhausted from the week's activities, but Morgan and Erin were excited about the end of the year festivities as school had adjourned for the summer. Morgan had graduated from high school. It had been a whirlwind of events that included choir concerts, school performances, prom, school dances and luncheons for parents, Awards Night, a cotillion, and class trips. Erin had her schedule of school events as well, but fully supported her older sister. And there I was trying to get through the final year of ministry preparation and seminary, while being a high school teacher closing out Final Exams at my school. My house and dining room table was filled with my books, their books, computers, and projects everywhere. Somehow, we came in each evening and picked up where we had left off. And this night was no different than the others. Morgan had her driver's license, and she was to drive one of the family cars to visit friends from school, with her sister Erin. They were not allowed to let anyone else get into the car. They were going to watch movies, eat pizza and be back home before 11:00 p.m. After putting some curls in their hair, I kissed them both as they went out the door, and said, "luv ya." Morgan was already out of the door and Erin turned and said, "Mom, I know that, why do you have to kiss me every time I go out the door? I am not a baby anymore. I am going to the eleventh grade." I smiled and kissed her anyway.

My Daughter

Every mother has at least one child who clings to her. This is the one who wants to leap in your bed every night, brings all her dolls and books and snacks and climbs in your bed, then turns on the latest edition of her favorite show and goes to sleep with crumbs everywhere when you wake up. Well that was my Erin.

As a toddler, if I walked out of the room, she cried. If I answered the phone, she cried. When I left her at school on the first day she cried. I never knew if I had traumatized her just by going to the bathroom or not! She was just that kind of child. In contrast, my firstborn was independent from birth. She sat up too soon, rolled over too soon, walked too soon and ran rather than walked. She was always running in the other direction. Not Erin, she was usually running towards me.

I always pictured her being the child who would grow up, marry and raise a family right down the street from her parents. She was easy to get along with, quiet in her own right, but she said what she meant, and would walk away. I can't recall chastising Erin for anything other than losing her gloves, hat, library books and lunch money.

She was the teacher's pet, had excellent grades, loved music and playing instruments, she had great friends and loved sleeping in my lap at church. Her sister Morgan was a self-starter, had an opinion about everything, was usually called upon to organize an activity at school, was very organized and approached the necessity of education in direct correlation to her degree of love for the teacher. Talk about contrasts!

NICOLE S. MASON, ESQUIRE

The Knock on the Door from Law Enforcement

At about 11:00 p.m., I dozed off to sleep while waiting for the girls to come in. I heard a knock on the door from my bedroom, assumed that it was the girls. I waited to hear them come up the stairs. A moment passed, then I heard nothing. My husband then came into the bedroom with a dazed looked on his face. I asked him if something was wrong. He couldn't speak. I yelled out "What is wrong?" All he could say was Erin! What about Erin? I ran into the living room with him trailing me thinking that maybe Erin had fallen or hurt herself. He whispered as loud as he could that she had died. With no life in my body, I hit the floor. I could feel my chest tighten and there was no air. I was choking. Could I be in a bad dream? Was I still asleep? I looked around the room, and my husband was on the floor as well. Was he sure? Who had been at my door? Where was my other daughter? Had they been together? "Where is my daughter?," I screamed. We laid on the floor for moments that seemed like hours, writhing in speechless chest-gripping, mind-numbing agony.

Then my phone rang. It was my other daughter, saying that she could not reach her sister. Her phone kept ringing, but Erin never answered. I told her to come home, immediately. She did not grasp the tone of my voice and replied that she would rather wait for Erin. I told her, that I would explain things to her when she got home. I called my neighbor to come over to help me gather my thoughts. I was in pajamas, and a bonnet. I knew the house would fill quickly with family and friends. I could barely talk but called as many as I had on speed dial. I couldn't remember anyone's number. The police sent a car to take us to the hospital to view her body. Another couple we knew met us at the hospital, along with my sisters-in-law.

As we entered that hospital room, I refused to believe that she was dead. I called her name, as she lay lifeless on the metal table. I called God to raise her up as he had raised Jairus' daughter in Matthew 9:18-26. I cried out to God in a loud voice. I yelled out, "Get up Erin! Get up Erin, in the name of Jesus Christ!" But the will of God had spoken. I slumped into a chair in the room while my family cried over her body. What could possibly be the plan of God for this family that He should allow one so full of life to be taken?

When we returned home, I asked Morgan why the two of them were not together that night as they had been told. She said that when they all met up with friends from school, they went to get fast food in different vehicles; some had ordered Chinese, others had not. Erin got in the car with a young man that we did not know well. She had never been allowed to ride with anyone but family until she got in the car with him on that night. The car in which Erin was a passenger was struck on the passenger's side by two other teen drivers. They all had cell phones in their hands and no seat belts. She was killed instantly; her neck was broken. The young man driving was in critical condition and was hospitalized at another hospital. The driver that hit them and his passenger did not sustain any serious injuries.

My Community's Response

At the time of Erin's passing, my husband and I belonged to two different churches. We had served together for a time, but as I moved farther in my seminary studies, I interned at another church in the inner city and joined that church. Our children attended both churches. My husband sang in the choir at the former church and had no intentions of leaving his choir. We literally had two churches who mourned for us and with us. There was a steady stream of food, cards, calls, flowers, cooks, attendants and visitors for the next two weeks. I wish I could say that I found comfort in my husband, but you must understand how grief works. Two broken people have a very difficult time consoling one another. My husband was not an expressive man in an intimate way. He could joke around but did not really know how to express his inward thoughts. You could be lonely just sitting with him, even when things were okay. Grief drove a wedge between us that was more like a chasm.

My pastor visited and sat with us for hours. My husband's pastor visited as well. We reached out to the high school that our children attended, and the principal of the school came over to be with us. The school clubs in which my daughters were affiliated were notified of Erin's death, and those teens began to come by with their parents to express their sorrow. Some of the young people were so distraught that their parents would only allow them to stay for a brief period.

My Marriage

Every marriage has its trials, and my marriage was no exception. Two people coming together who are from totally different backgrounds, are bound to struggle as they reach for common ground that will be forged in unity. We had differing views on communication, finances, child-rearing, the role of extended family, education, women and careers—let's just say we differed. My approach to daily living is to tackle concerns; my spouse lived around the concern, keeping his views hidden until they were surfaced forcefully. When you suffer the loss of a child, your emotions, personality and worldviews scream aloud to each other and everyone connected to your situation! We do not all grieve the same way. When your situation is exposed for other mourners, neighbors, spectators, saints, "aints," and skeptics to examine, you can only respond based on who you are and not who and what people think of you and their expectations.

I could not tell from day to day what my husband was feeling. I could only share my emotions to a limit; I turned to other women of the marriage ministry in which I served, as well as to a small number of ministers who had lost children who reached out to me. I am told that quite often men feel a need to fix things when they are broken; this could not be fixed, therefore a retreat on my husband's part was apropos, coupled with his normal demeanor of avoidance. And I simply lacked the spiritual and mental fortitude to engage any farther than my daily requirements just to survive, and not sink into despair and depression.

Decisions, Decisions

Each morning that I arose I had to shake off the numbness, so I could think through decisions that were critical to planning a funeral. The medical examiner called for an autopsy, which I refused because I could not bear the thought of someone cutting my child's body. I was told that it was due process because of the nature of the accident, and I had to agree with their request. We had to select a coffin, among other things. A constant parade of people needed me to make a decision about this thing or that thing.

A friend whose children had grown-up with mine, came over each day and said the simplest of things to snap me out of the numbness. She said, "Did you check the mail?" "Did you eat today?" "Have you done the laundry this week?" "You have quite a few messages you need to check." One day she said, "You need to exert some physical energy," and off to the local pool I went to thrash the water, cry and to feel the effect of water surrounding me. She took time from her husband and sons to come by every day to keep me mentally engaged in the daily process of living. I thank her and her husband to this day and will forever remember how important it was for someone to keep the daily cognitive activities of remembering that I still had a house to keep in order.

Grief

Grief can feel like a heavy blanket that shrouds its wearer. It doesn't fit, but just hangs all over you. It is with you when you rise, and as you go through your day. It is there as you lay down. It is important that you wear it for a while, lest you move beyond your pain too soon. Although you may never understand the purpose of the entire situation, why it occurred and even how it could have happened, when you put every precaution in place—please, please, please appreciate the experience of being fully human enough to feel pain and cry your heart out. When Jesus, our Lord, heard that Lazarus had died, he wept, full of deep sorrow. Martha blames him, saying if he had come earlier, the whole thing could have been avoided and her brother would be sitting at the table eating a meal with them all. (See John 11:21) One note here, like Martha, you will encounter people who will respond just as she did "If you had done . . . your daughter would still be alive." As cruel as this sounds, it happened to our Lord—it can happen to us, and it happened to me. And ironically, just days before Erin's death, I stood before my congregation and was anointed by my Bishop as a Minister of the Gospel at Greater Mt. Calvary Holy Church. Shortly thereafter,

I had to bury my daughter; it was a mountain-top experience that later lead me to the valley!

Emerging From the Ashes

One of the best ways that I could create a lasting memory and tribute to my daughter was to start a scholarship fund to honor who she was an excellent student, musician, liturgical dancer, cheerleader, and writer. There were so many young people who had become a part of my life because of both my daughters, I wanted a way to keep her memory fresh in the hearts and minds of others, and to help pay for the education of those coming behind her who embraced learning and enjoyed life as much as she did.

Several couples we knew joined with us to establish the Erin Ashleigh Mercer Scholarship Foundation, which had a two-fold purpose: To bring awareness to Teen Driver Safety and to help fund the education of young people who exemplified the character and the many gifts of Erin. We held a banquet each year to raise funds for a few years, and we awarded scholarships in Maryland and New Jersey where my father lived, because he wanted to participate in some way at his church. To date we have awarded 20 scholarships, with two international students receiving it in the past two years. Most of our donors are private now, and the Scholarship is managed through Bishop McNamara High School in Maryland. It will remain a part of my family's life for the rest of my life, and I have left instructions in my Last Will and Testament for my daughter Morgan to continue it after I am gone.

Getting past grief and loss takes time, effort, patience and a daily intentionality to embrace life differently. You learn to allow yourself to be present in the moment. If a memory hits you that day, let it! Cry or journal or call a friend and talk, but don't stay there. This is where many people become stuck; the focus can become off-balanced with too many thoughts of yesterday. If you can trust God, if you can lean into Him, He will lead you into a "new normal." This doesn't mean that you forget about what has happened; it means you embrace it as a *part* of your life's story. There will be other chapters to live and tell about.

Death can bring a crisis of faith, but with each crisis a new level of faith can emerge, and a greater understanding of the Divine Providence of God can be embraced-a kind of blessed assurance. A professor at Wesley Theological Seminary introduced me to a book called, *The Message of the Psalms*, by Walter Brueggemann, which opened my mind and heart to the many words of faith written in the Bible to comfort, to heal, to query, to lament and to build trust after walking through the valley of the shadow of death. I have since embraced the Psalms as an anthem for the emotional and spiritual tsunamis in my life, and I encourage others to as well.

What God?

The years following Erin's death brought me to have a series of dreams about the young man who was driving the car that Erin had ridden in that night. I could see his face clearly. I felt that perhaps I was dreaming out of repressed anger, but the dreams had a different tone, and as I arose from the dream one morning, I prayed to God for an answer to them. It became clear to me what was before me.

To Be Continued...

Conclusion

After reading these powerful testimonies of the authors in this book, I am confident that your faith in God has increased and the fire in your soul has not only been ignited, but it is an inferno. I want to encourage you to take the time to examine your life and tap into those pivotal points and life-altering moments that have shaped who you are and consider sharing them others. Many people in the world need hope that things will get better in their lives. It is the overcoming testimonies in our lives that help to increase the good in the world and decrease the negative.

If you have a desire to share your testimony and you have never authored a book, I would love to work with you to help you share your testimony with the world. Send an email to contact@nicolesmason.com and put the following in the subject line: ***Faith For Fiery Trials – Share My Story.***

Meet the Co-Authors

Debbie Andrews is an Administrative Specialist with the Federal Government, breast cancer survivor, and advocate. www.facebook.com/debbie.andrewsjohnson

Rhonda Bunch-Turner is a mother, grandmother, and she loves to write, travel and spending time with family and friends. www.facebook.com/rhonda.bunch

Minister Taneshia Curry is a mom, minister and anointed psalmist that has served as a backup singer for Tramaine Hawkins, Martha Munizzi and Maurette Brown-Clark, to name a few.
www.facebook.com/taneshia.curry.5

NICOLE S. MASON, ESQUIRE

Renee Dantzler is a wife to her high school sweetheart, Douglas Dantzler, mom, grandmother, and certified fitness trainer. www.facebook.com.naedantz

Minister Mary Harris is a mom, grandmother and minister. She is the founder of Dvine Beauti, an organization that brings awareness to domestic violence. www.facebook.com/dvinebeauti2015

Dr. Mary J. Huntley is a wife of 44 years to Dr. Ronald Lee Huntley. They serve together at Trinity Global Empowerment Ministries. Dr. Huntley is the recipient of numerous awards for her life-changing work in the community. She also serves as a coach, mentor, and counselor. www.trinitygem.org

Kisha Martin-Burney is a wife, mom, grandmother and award winning real estate agent in Maryland.
www.dmvrealestatediva.com

Elder Cheryl Mercer is a wife, mom, minister and Clergy Ambassador to the United States Attorney's Office and advocate for women in prison. She serves as the Board Chair at the Fairview Reentry Center in Washington, DC. Elder Mercer is also the founder of Women of Worth Fellowship International Ministries.
www.wwfim.org

FAITH FOR FIERY TRIALS

Elder Angela Minor is an attorney, professor and minister. She is the owner and co-founder of Minor & Willcox Law Firm. She is also the Director of the Martin Luther King, Jr. Forensics Program that consists of a debate team and a mock trial team. Elder Minor has led her teams to national championships.
www.minorwillcoxlaw.com

Tracey Simms Washington is a mom, Contract Officer in the Federal Government and founder and President of the Simms Scholarship Foundation. She is also a co-owner of AJW Property Acquisitions, LLC, a real estate investment business, with her son.
www.facebook.com/tswashington1

Meet the Celebrity Authors

Charlotte Avery is a wife, mom of 7, speaker, author, entrepreneur, blogger and the founder of the Being Charlotte Avery brand. Using her #PhDinMotherhood, she helps women blend their lives by loving themselves, strengthening their families, living authentically and doing it all in style!
www.beingcharlotteavery.com

Crystal Y. Davis is a speaker, coach, consultant, and entrepreneur. She is the founder & CEO of The Lean Coach, Inc. She is a certified Lean Six Sigma Black Belt and a certified Leadership Coach. Additionally, Crystal is the founder of DisruptHER™, where she is teaching women how to succeed in male dominated environments. www.theleancoachinc.com

NICOLE S. MASON, ESQUIRE

Pastor Joyce Gilmer is an author, speaker, and Dream Activation Coach™, consultant and entrepreneur. She is the founder & CEO of Empowered Living Coaching and Consulting. Pastor Joyce helps women Wake Up to their dreams. www.joycegilmer.com

Minister SharRon Jamison is an entrepreneur, author, speaker, visionary, life strategist and corporate leader. She is the founder & CEO of The Jamison Group, a leadership training and development company specializing in personal transformation and relational healing. Minister Jamison challenges her clients to Dare to Soar Higher!
www.sharronjamison.com

Dr. Vikki Johnson is a best-selling author, mentor, coach, visionary, TEDx speaker, Chaplain, minister and founder of Soul Wealth™ Academy. She is the founder & CEO of Authentic Living Enterprises, LLC. She helps women break up with the status quo in their lives to live with clarity, confidence and self-worth. www.vikkijohnson.com

Minister Beverly Lucas is a mom, grandmother, author, minister, College Administrator, and professor. She is the recipient of numerous awards. Minister Lucas is also the founder & CEO of Heart Xpressions, Inc.,

the premier line of women's inspirational cards and spiritual literature.
www.facebook.com/beverly.feltonlucas

Bershan Shaw is an author, international speaker, coach, breast cancer survivor, entrepreneur and founder of urawarrior.com. She helps women find their inner warrior. www.bershan.com

About the Visionary

Elder Nicole S. Mason is a wife to her college sweetheart, mom to three sons, minister, best-selling author, attorney, executive leadership coach, international speaker, international radio show host, entrepreneur and trailblazing senior leader. Elder Mason is known as the "Leader's Leader" for her truth, sage advice and spiritual insight she offers to women leaders. She is the recipient of numerous awards. Elder Mason has served in various leadership roles in ministry and the marketplace.
www.nicolesmason.com

Other Books by Elder Nicole S. Mason

- Monday Morning Motivations: Encouraging Words to Start Your Week

- Morning Meditations: Starting Your Day with Passion, Purpose, and Power

- Meditaciones Matinales: Comenzando Tu Día Con Proposito Pasión Y Poder

Contributing Author

- What Is A Courageous Woman: A Collaborative Book Featuring 78 Co-Authors Celebrating Courageous Women by Telishia Berry

- Glambitious Guide to Greatness: How to Go from Doubt to Destiny & from Surviving to Thriving by Glam Boss Organization

- Behind the Scenes of a Phenomenal Woman: Featuring Stories of 24 Phenomenal Women by Dr. Chantelle Teasdell

NICOLE S. MASON, ESQUIRE

- Women Inspiring Nations: 25 Women Sharing Their Stories and Gifts to Inspire and Transform Lives Across Nations by Cheryl Wood

- Igniting the Fire: A Woman's Guide to Setting a Blaze in Ministry, Business, and Life by LaTracey Copeland Hughes

- The Fearless Living Experience: Bold and Empowered Women Share Their Triumph Over Life's Curveballs by Cheryl Wood